PRAISE FOR
YOU'RE GETTING DIVORCED... NOW WHAT?

"You're Getting Divorced...Now What? is a wonderful resource filled with helpful tools designed to assist those going through the Divorce Journey. It provides insights into the emotional rollercoaster involved in divorce and gives the reader numerous resources to help manage those emotions. Real life stories not only illustrate how each experience varies, but also gives the reader a sense of community, support, and the knowledge that they are not in this experience alone. In this book, Sandra's compassion, expertise, and ability to write in a clear and understandable manner shine through brilliantly. I highly recommend this book for anyone contemplating or going through a divorce."
  - Joelle A. Perez, Esq., *Peacemaker Divorce Mediation*

"This is a good read for those in need of sound divorce advice. Sandra has shared the knowledge she has gained through her years of experience in divorce court. You're *Getting Divorced...Now What?* will help you get through what can be the most painful life choice for any couple, especially with a family."
  - Debbie Leon, *divorced mother of two*

"You're Getting Divorced…Now What? is the perfect book should you find yourself needing to litigate your divorce. Sandra helps you identify the myriad of emotions one goes through and helps you plan and prepare for what lies ahead. Easy to follow forms will keep you organized and first-hand accounts help you to realize you are not alone."

   - Chris Pulitano, *New Beginnings Divorce Mediation*

"If you are about to go through a divorce, tighten your chinstrap because it's a rough road ahead. *You're Getting Divorced…Now What?* has the sound advice that you need to get you through it."

   - Michael ScottoDimaso, *divorced father of two*

"You're Getting Divorced…Now What? not only guides you through the processes of selecting an attorney, what not to say to the children, and what to expect from the judges, but it's also compassionate and reassuring. Although you are going through a very challenging time in your life, you are not alone, Sandra Radna is with you."

   - Marci Brockmann, *satisfied former client and author of Permission to Land: Searching for Love, Home & Belonging*

"You're Getting Divorced…Now What? covers everything! Emotions, checklists, finances, expectations, relatability and so much more. Wow. I can't even imagine how this would've changed the hell I went through. Reading it invoked some painful emotions for me…but I'm happy for the many who will benefit from it. It will be life changing!!!!"

   - Christy Smith, *divorced mother of two*

YOU'RE GETTING DIVORCED... NOW WHAT?

The Ultimate Divorce Court Guide

What you can't find on
Google™ or learn from your friends

SANDRA M. RADNA, ESQ.

First published by Ultimate World Publishing 2020
Copyright © 2020 Sandra M. Radna, ESQ.

ISBN

Paperback - 978-1-922372-52-9
Ebook - 978-1-922372-53-6

Cover design: Ultimate World Publishing
Layout and typesetting: Ultimate World Publishing
Editor: Hayley Ward
Front Cover photo: howcolour-Shutterstock.com (Divorce Law)

Ultimate World Publishing
Diamond Creek,
Victoria Australia 3089
www.writeabook.com.au

"People need to know this...You should put it all in a book."

Thank you Christy, Ed, Elena, Tom, Erika, Michael and my clients who allowed me to share their experiences in this book.

CONTENTS

YOU'RE GETTING DIVORCED...
NOW WHAT?

INTRODUCTION

If you're reading this book, you're probably a member of a club that nobody wants to be part of - *the divorce court club*. To be a member of this club, you must either be going through or have gone through a divorce, custody, or child support issue. None of these issues are fun and none of them are pretty. You are likely in the court system because your issues could not be resolved any other way.

No one gets married with the intention of getting divorced. And no one has children planning to go to court to fight over custody, child support or parenting time. Unfortunately, if you are in court for any of these issues, you are there because you felt that you were left with no other choice. When you meet someone who is going through, or has gone through this process, you feel an instant connection because that person *gets it*. They know what it's like. They've been through the war. Just like you have. And they probably have P.T.S.D. flashbacks whenever someone mentions the words "judge" or "court". They wear the battle scars of docket numbers, court transcripts and court orders with the raised seal. They know what it's like to be demoralized by a judge or by a court officer. They know what it's like to wait in a noisy, crowded hallway for hours only to learn that your case has been postponed to another date for a reason you don't quite understand.

I am a divorce attorney who has been practicing for over 25 years. I have directly experienced many of the different situations that people who are going through divorce encounter.

This book is written to prepare you for the frustration, shock, hurt and disillusionment that affect people who go through the divorce court system without the armor of knowledge. The aim of this book is to familiarize you with the process of going through a contested or litigated divorce and to prepare you for what to expect in court. Before ever stepping foot in a courtroom, you should know how to select an attorney, what to say versus what not to say to the children, and what to expect from the judges. To achieve this level of understanding, you will require information beyond what Google™, advice from friends, or a one-hour consultation with an attorney will provide to you. Your situation is unique, and you must know what will help you specifically.

This book is the resource that will help guide you through your divorce. Each chapter explains what to expect and how to prepare for divorce court by utilizing real-life stories. Additionally, you will be given practical tools, steps and strategies for your situation. Now, I know we are all busy, and things are especially hectic when you are going through a divorce, but don't worry because this book is not intended for you to read in one sitting. You can refer to the sections that apply to your circumstances, as you need them. Although every chapter in this book may not be applicable right now, it is a useful guide for when various situations arise.

Take a deep breath: no matter how impossible your situation might seem, most cases eventually get resolved, and yours will too!

CHAPTER 1

FEAR, SHAME, GUILT, SADNESS...OR JUST PISSED OFF

"It is the moment you realize that you left without ever leaving. It is the moment that you realize that fear, shame and guilt are the only things standing in the way of the life God meant for you to live."
- Shannon L. Alder

Every divorce is filled with emotion, especially in the beginning. However, as you might guess, not everyone experiences the same emotions. The emotions one feels can vary depending on a number of factors, such as whose decision it was to get divorced and the circumstances surrounding what precipitated your divorce. There is an important distinction between the emotions you experience when you are just *thinking* about divorce, and the

1

emotions you feel when you *actually decide* to divorce. Once you make the decision to get divorced, everything becomes very real. You are really getting divorced. Once you grasp that it's actually happening, you have this "deer in the headlights" moment where you almost feel like time stops. You realize that from the moment you commit to the decision to divorce, life, as it existed during your marriage, will be irreversibly changed. And, naturally, the idea of change triggers many emotions.

Most often, the emotions experienced by those going through divorce are fear, shame, guilt, sadness, or anger. This is because in almost every situation when you decided to get married you made a lifelong commitment and did not expect the marriage to end in divorce. You thought everything would work out and be great. And, of course you did. Who doesn't? Yet, here you are - feeling guilty or ashamed for deciding to get divorced, or fearful about what will happen once you tell people you're getting divorced, or sad about the loss of the life you were supposed to have, or pissed off because of the betrayal by your spouse.

Any human being is going to feel some type of emotion when the relationship that was supposed to last "forever" ends. This is normal. You are not alone. And know this: there is strength in community. The decision to divorce is so private. Even though you know in your heart that this is what you are going to do, most people will be very selective about with whom to discuss it. However, the pages in this book will give you the community that you need and desire. Throughout this book, you will hear accounts of people who have traveled the roads and made it through the journey from B.D. (Before Divorce) to A.D. (After Divorce). Traveling through this book with your Fellow Divorce Warriors (FDWs) will you give you a sense of community that is different from what you may already have with your friends and family. Your FDWs will share their experiences with you. Through the process of reading and learning from their experiences, you will feel supported when you are feeling emotional, you will become aware of potential obstacles you may face during your own D.J. (Divorce Journey), and you will learn how to persevere and protect yourself, your children and your finances. So, now your D.J. begins. Here are some examples of how your FDWs felt when they decided to get divorced[1]:

FEAR

ALISON

> *When I decided to get divorced, I was afraid to be a young single mother. So many people told me not to marry my husband, but I didn't listen. I married him and hoped my marriage would last forever. And now I was getting divorced. I was embarrassed. I was sad for my children and, despite the pain my husband had caused us due to his substance abuse, I still hoped he would recover from his addiction and be a present and good father. My biggest fear was that he would abandon our children, but if he stayed in their lives, I was worried that he would put them in harm's way. It was a no-win situation at the time. I thought about finances and who would help with my children when I went back to work. I didn't have family nearby. I was afraid of my husband because of his drug use and abusive actions towards me. My fear stopped me in my tracks and it took me some time to gather the courage to move forward. Despite all of that though, once I made the decision to get divorced, I was relieved. I could see this light at the end of the tunnel. I truly believed that once we were divorced, my children would no longer be exposed to all of the conflict surrounding my husband's drug use. The*

---

[1] All of the stories in this book are real-life accounts of situations experienced by the author's clients, with their consent. When requested, names were changed for privacy.

divorce would allow them to live in an environment that was happy and peaceful instead of tense and uncomfortable. Once I made the decision to get divorced, there was no turning back. With hard work, determination and resolve, everything fell into place for me and my children. It was the right decision. My kids are great now, even though we all suffered because of what my now former husband did to us.

SHAME

DEIRDRE

I had been in an awful marriage where I was lied to and cheated on, yet I stuck around because I didn't want to be the "divorced girl". I had gotten pregnant before I was married so I already felt embarrassed about that and I stuck around in this awful relationship. Even after I asked my husband to leave, I lied to my family and my friends for a month. I lived by myself and I made up stories for why people couldn't come over, or where my husband was when they came over because I didn't want to be "a failure". I didn't want to let down my parents who had done so much for me and my ex-husband. After a month of hiding everything from everybody and living completely alone and dealing with everything by myself, I approached my parents and I apologized to them. For failing them. For letting them down. For not being able to make my marriage work. I cried and I apologized for being an embarrassment to them. They cried back and they looked at me, held me and said, "What did we ever do wrong as parents that we would make you feel that you should be sorry or ashamed for getting yourself out of a bad situation?" They just hugged me and held me. That was my breakthrough after a month by myself and entirely dealing with my emotions alone until I finally had the courage to tell people the truth.

Everybody accepted me with open arms and supported me. I never had to be afraid, I never had to be alone, I never had to cry, I didn't have to feel embarrassed, but I did until everyone told me that it was ok.

GUILT

BRAD

When I decided to get divorced, I felt as if I failed. I felt like, here's the most important relationship in my life, to that point anyway, and it's over. I mean of course there was blame to go around or I could actually have said it was this person's fault, or that person's fault, but it was my fault, too. It was my marriage and now it was ending. I felt low and horrified. It was a terrible, terrible feeling. The children were the hardest part. I had it ingrained in me my whole life that a "normal family" was a mother, father, kids. I had this image in my head that this was the way life should go. I thought the kids would grow up and then they would leave, and my wife and I would grow old and then we would become grandparents and so on and so forth. I had this kind of Norman Rockwell view of the world. And now that was all gone. I felt like I kind of tore this life out from under my children. There was this potential of this kind of picturesque picket fence life and I kind of took it from them. And then everything that goes along with that. Then there was the thought of other people judging me. First, I worried about how they were going to feel about me. Even people that were not that important to me. That was the odd part. I remember being concerned about how the neighbors would feel. I didn't even talk to my neighbors. And I was worried about what they would think. How they would see me. Never mind the important people in my life like my parents. Was I going to take years off of their lives because of my divorce? How were they going to deal with it? Then there were my siblings. What would they think? I felt like people had enough stuff to deal with in their lives and now, they had to deal with my stuff too. I worried about the life that I was taking away from my children and the life that I was taking away from myself. But in the end, divorce was the right decision. I'm happier, my children are happier, and my family is happy that I am no longer in that difficult marriage.

SADNESS

JANET

We had been married for 27 years. There was a lot of fighting throughout our marriage. Ups and downs. Highs and lows. Towards the end of our marriage, my husband's verbal abuse towards me got worse. He was also verbally abusive to our children. I handled it throughout our marriage. We stayed together and tried to work it out. But in the end, it became too much for me, and I decided to get divorced. Even though it was my decision to get divorced, and even though I knew it was the right thing for me to do to have the life that I wanted, I was just so sad. I could not stop crying. The crying was ridiculous and confusing to me because I knew with every ounce of my being that it was the right decision. This was something that I had to do. I needed peace in my life. I couldn't continue walking around on eggshells never knowing what was going to set him off and what we would be fighting about next. He kept begging me to get back together, but then he would say horrible, mean things to me. I received confirmation after confirmation that it was the right decision to move forward with the divorce, but I cried an ocean of tears and felt like I was in this mountain of sadness. Until one day my attorney explained to me that I wasn't crying about leaving my current situation. I was crying about losing what I thought my marriage was going to be. Which it never was. And that changed everything. It made me stop crying. Not that by itself, of course. I also went to therapy and did other things for my mental health. But that realization that I was crying for what should have been, but never was, gave me clarity and strength to move on.

PISSED OFF

TONY

I suspected that my wife was having an affair. When she found out that I suspected it, instead of trying to work our marriage out, she turned on me and asked me for a divorce. I had a whole life with her. Over 25 years of marriage. I was a good husband. I provided for my family. I provided for my children. I was present for them. I gave my wife a good life. She never worked. She stayed home with the children - something that I knew that she wanted, and I was happy to provide for her. I gave my wife and our children a beautiful house and a beautiful neighborhood in a great school district. I supported them and helped my children so that they would do well athletically and academically. I did nothing to hurt my wife. But in the divorce, all she tried to do was destroy me. She made up lies about me. She went to my job, repeatedly, and told them that I physically abused her! Since I worked at a school with children, they asked me to leave the job that I loved. She did everything that she could to make my life miserable. She turned my children away from me. Throughout the beginning of the divorce I was just so angry at the life that she took away from me. I felt like I couldn't see straight. My lawyer helped me to focus and get through it. Looking back is still painful, but I am so grateful that the divorce is done and over.

7

GET YOUR MIND RIGHT

As you can see, everyone has a different emotional experience when they make the decision to get divorced. Your feelings surrounding your decision to divorce, or your acceptance of the fact that you are getting divorced are unique to your situation. This book is here to assure you that whatever feelings you have, *they are normal and part of the process.* The most common emotions associated with getting divorced are guilt and shame, especially when there are children involved. Even though the emotions are common and to be expected, be aware that you are not able to make your best decisions while you're in the middle of beating yourself up, which is the common reaction when people are feeling guilty or ashamed. You also are not able to make your best decisions when you are filled with fear, sadness, or anger. That's why there are expressions like "paralyzed with fear," "debilitating sadness," and "blind rage". It is absolutely necessary for you to acknowledge and name the emotions you are feeling, understand why you are feeling them, and then move forward so that you may have a productive relationship with your divorce attorney[2] which will result in a more satisfactory outcome for your divorce.

Let's unpack what I just said. Whatever your emotions are, it is imperative that you address them so that you can plan. You cannot think clearly when you're upset, sad or angry about whatever it is that you've experienced. It's just a fact. You cannot concentrate when your head is filled with emotions. I'm not saying that you're not going to be emotional throughout this divorce. You absolutely will be. You will run the gamut of every emotion there is. But in order to plan effectively, and achieve your goals, you must act with a clear head. That means putting your emotions aside (at least temporarily) so you can *make a plan.*

---

[2] Throughout this book, the words "lawyer" and "attorney" are used interchangeably as they are synonymous.

If you go to this link, www.radnalaw.com/YGDNW/forms, you will find that I have created forms for you to utilize throughout your D.J. to get your thoughts and your divorce plan organized. The GET YOUR MIND RIGHT© form found at: www. radnalaw.com/YGDNW/forms/GetYourMindRight will help you to identify your emotions. You can print it out if you prefer to write, or you can download it to your computer and type on the form.[3] On the form, write down or type in the emotions that you are experiencing. Is it fear, shame, guilt, sadness, anger, or a combination of some or all of those emotions? The form asks you to identify what is causing you to feel those emotions. This part is optional. For some people, delving into the causes behind certain emotions will be helpful, while for others it will not be. The most important thing is to acknowledge that you are having those emotions and to identify each emotion by name. Once you name the emotions you are experiencing you can work on getting your mind right. On the form you will be asked what the emotions you are feeling cause you to do. For example, Janet told us that her sadness caused her to cry, Deirdre told us that her shame caused her to hide, Alison said that her fear stopped her in her tracks and Tony said that he was so angry he couldn't see straight. Once you identify what your feelings are and what they are causing you to do, then you can work to manage them effectively.

WHY?

So why am I having you do all of this? Going through a divorce is serious work. You are making some tough decisions that will affect your future and, if you have children, their lives as well. If you do not properly and effectively manage your emotions, you may make decisions that you would not have made if you had

---

[3] Before you put anything about your divorce on your computer, make sure your spouse does not have access to your computer by changing your passwords and password protecting anything concerning your divorce.

been in control of your emotions. To decide how your life will be A.D., you must have a clear head. You have to "get your mind right". And these forms will help you do just that.

But why the fear, shame, guilt, sadness, and anger? Alison, Deirdre, Brad, Janet, and Tony told you the facts of their situation which caused them to feel the way that they did. But what about you? To move forward, the question must be answered.

In addition to the particular circumstances of what brought you to the decision to divorce, the norms in our culture explain why it is so common for divorcing people to feel this way. The expectation of what a marriage and family should be is part of our American culture. As children we read and watch fairy tales about the prince and princess who find each other and live happily ever after. Happily ever after is what we all want. And when we have children, happily ever after is what we want for them. But, hey, *life happens*. And the fact is, happily ever after is not the same for everyone. And that's okay. It means different things to different people.

This is not a psychology book, and it is not meant to be. It is a book about what happens in divorce court. The fact is that the beginning of your divorce is the ending of your marriage, which is not something that can be ignored. Even though you know in your heart of hearts that getting a divorce is the right decision for you, most people feel sad about losing, not the marriage that they are choosing to leave, but the marriage they thought that they were going to have when they first got married. Or they are pissed off because the life they were supposed to have, planned to have, and worked to maintain, is now being taken away from them.

Prior to comprehending that the loss you are mourning, or are angry about, is the marriage you *thought* you had or were supposed to have, not the marriage that you *actually* had, your emotions are confusing. You feel conflicted. Even though you know that your divorce is necessary because the situation you're in is no longer livable or enjoyable, you may feel guilty because it didn't work out, or ashamed because you are concerned about what other people will think of you. It doesn't make sense. It makes you feel like you're losing your mind. But, once you accept that your guilt, shame, sadness, and anger are linked to your idea of what your marriage was supposed to have been and not what it actually was, you will see that your mindset shifts. *You will have clarity and you will be ready to plan.*

But how can you possibly plan? Every part of your plan for your A.D. life brings up a new emotion. Well, you do it the way you've done anything in your life that you've had to get through. You give yourself some time to be fearful, guilty, ashamed, sad or angry and then you make the decision to set your emotions aside, focus and plan. If you are having a hard time getting a handle on your emotions (and there are many very good and valid reasons why this may be the case) you should consider seeing a therapist or a divorce coach. *There is no shame in asking for help.* Acknowledging that you need help is one of the most important steps in the process. It is only after the acknowledgement that you can take the next step.

In order to help you focus, utilize the MY REASONS© form found at www.radnalaw.com/YGDNW/forms/MyReasons. The form has two columns. The heading on one column is: "REASONS TO DIVORCE." The heading on the other column is "REASONS TO STAY MARRIED." Everyone's list is going to be different. Only you can determine what goes in each of those columns. If you're reading this book, I'll take a guess and say that the column with the reasons that you should be getting divorced is probably longer than the column with the reasons to stay married. Sometimes it's not your decision to get a divorce, it's your spouse's decision. In that case, your REASONS TO DIVORCE column might be short. Unfortunately, if your spouse no longer wishes to be married, commenced a divorce and served you with divorce papers, you are on a D.J. Similar to those who decided to begin a divorce action, this form will help you focus and make the best decisions for yourself moving forward.

When happily ever after isn't what your marriage turned out to be, and you decide to divorce, you need reassurance. Examining column one, REASONS TO DIVORCE, should help you realize that your reasons for deciding to divorce are solid. You've probably had many sleepless nights before you finally came to this decision. The only one living your life is you and you are the only one who knows the true story of what was happening in your marriage. This was not a decision that was made on a whim. But, to paraphrase what Eckhart Tolle said so eloquently in "A New Earth,"[4] too much of our life is spent being upset about something that happened in the past or being worried about something that may happen in the future, when the only thing we have control over is the present.[5] You cannot change the past. And worrying about the future turns into paralyzing fear. Once you recognize that you can't change what happened in the past, and that there's no point being fearful about a future that may or may not happen, you can allow yourself to let go of any fear, shame, guilt, sad or angry feelings that you have. Once you let go, it's time to push forward and plan.

THE PLAN

So, now that you understand your emotions, and you know you made the right decision in committing to get divorced, how do you plan? Where do you begin? Although every situation is unique, you will usually have to figure out the following: where you will live, who will the children live with primarily,

---

[4] Eckhart Tolle, A NEW EARTH, Awakening to Your Life's Purpose pages 114-121.
[5] This is my interpretation of a section of the book, A NEW EARTH, Awakening to Your Life's Purpose, not a direct quote.

how much money you will need to live on after the divorce and whether or not you need financial support from your spouse. The best way to figure this all out is to write it down (or type it out on your computer).

This does not have to be the final plan. This is just your initial plan. We will discuss the details of your plan throughout this book. But this initial plan will be your initial thoughts on how you want things to go. Go to: www.radnalaw.com/YGDNW/forms/InitialPlan. The INITIAL PLAN© form helps you lay out a plan, in broad strokes for your A.D. life. You will see that there are categories concerning where you will live, who your children will live with primarily and whether you require, or will be paying, spousal financial support. The form then has you go into more detail in each of those categories, even though it's just your initial plan.

WHERE WILL YOU LIVE?

If you and your spouse are currently living together, one of the first things you should think about is who will stay in the house and who will find a new place to live. If you would like to stay in the house that you lived in during the marriage (the marital residence), prepare a list of the costs associated with the house and determine whether you will have the financial ability to pay those costs. If you plan on moving out of the marital residence, and you want to get your own place, figure out how much money you need to do that. If you will be renting, research the costs of rents in the neighborhood in which you would like to live. If you want to purchase a residence, determine how much money you need to do so. If you want the children to live with you and you're going to be moving out of the marital residence, determine how many bedrooms you need. If your children are still school-aged, will you be residing in their current school district or will your children switch school districts when you move? Be aware that if you are switching school districts, you should speak with your children's other parent before making any final plans.

The INITIAL PLAN FORM© will also instruct you to make a list of both your current monthly expenses and your projected monthly expenses for after you or your spouse moves out of the marital residence.

Once you hire an attorney, he/she will advise you about the amount of child support and spousal support that you either will be receiving or paying. But, for purposes of this initial plan, it's fine for you to put in numbers that are 'guess-timates'.

WHERE WILL THE CHILDREN LIVE?

The most important decision that you and your spouse will make is where and with whom your children will live- you or your spouse. Sometimes it's an easy decision. For example, if one parent is working full-time and the other parent is home, it may make more sense for the children to be with the parent who is home. Sometimes it is not as clear cut. Maybe 50-50 custody makes sense for your situation. You should carefully review your circumstances to determine what is best for your children. Later in the book, we will discuss different situations to consider when determining where and with whom your children should live. For purposes of your initial plan, you should just indicate what you would like the custody plan to be and with whom you would like the children to live with primarily. You should also include in the plan what parenting time each parent will have.

FINANCIAL SUPPORT

During the marriage, it is likely that you shared the expenses. After the divorce, you will each be responsible for your own expenses. To determine the amount of money will require to be able to pay your monthly expenses A.D., refer to the list of your monthly expenses on your INITIAL PLAN© form. To this list add all of your bank accounts and assets, including real estate, cars, boats, businesses, brokerage accounts and retirement accounts. The INITIAL PLAN© form has categories for all of these items. Once you make your list, you will see your plan starting to materialize. This is just an overview of what your plan will be. *And it's also the beginning of your journey to your new life.*

Once you have completed your INITIAL PLAN©, you will have a good road map for moving forward with your divorce. And, congratulations! You've completed step one of your D.J.!

CHAPTER 2

TALK TO MY LAWYER

"...Lawyers smooth out difficulties, relieve stress, correct mistakes, take up other's burdens and by their efforts make possible the peaceful life of people in a peaceful state."

- John W. Davis

So now that you've made your INITIAL PLAN©, your next step is to hire an attorney. If you and your spouse agree on all issues, there are resources available for you to complete your divorce forms without the assistance of an attorney. Here is a link for all the courts in the United States: https://www.ncsc.org/information-and-resources/state-court-websites. Most courts in the United States have resources online to assist those who wish to proceed with their divorce without the assistance of an attorney. Completing the necessary forms can be time-consuming but is do-able by following the instructions on the court website. In a divorce in which you agree on all issues, it is unlikely that you will ever be required to appear before a judge. Your trips to court would be simply for the filing of papers, confirmation of what is contained in your divorce documents and retrieving your final Judgment of Divorce.

This book, however, is written for the situation which involves those whose D.J. (Divorce Journey) is not so straightforward. If you have a contested divorce - one in which you and your spouse do not agree to a number of issues - *it is strongly suggested that you hire an attorney to represent you*. The issues involved in a divorce are complicated and hiring an attorney to represent your interests will help you to better achieve your desired outcome. Throughout this book, I make references to topics you should discuss with your attorney. That is because an attorney who is experienced in the area of divorce law will be able to provide you with a wealth of information that you could not possibly know without a law degree coupled with experience. Attorneys have experience with the courthouse and the judges and they are familiar with the rules and procedures of the court. They know what is expected in divorce court. That will all be extremely helpful to you as you go through your D.J. and attempt to achieve your goals. If you represent yourself in a contested divorce, your D.J. will be much more complicated.

Hiring an attorney is one of the most important steps in the process of getting divorced. Your attorney, unlike your family and friends, will be able to give you a legal and enforceable solution when you have a problem in your divorce. You can talk to your friends regarding their divorces, but at the end of the day, your friends can only tell you what happened in *their* divorces, which are different from *your* divorce. Similarly, you can consult Google™, but Google™ does not understand your unique circumstances. Although there may be similarities between your divorce and your friend's divorce, such as both having a horrible spouse or having the same number of children, there are a variety of facts that will be different from your situation and likely to create a different outcome. No two divorces are alike, and it is important not to compare a friend's divorce to your own.

Your divorce attorney should be someone who will listen to you and strongly advocate for you. Choosing an attorney who is not right for you or your situation can have disastrous outcomes. In the following pages, I will give you steps to follow which will assist you in finding an attorney who is a good match for you and your situation. Here is what some of your FDWs (Fellow Divorce Warriors) experienced in their quest to find the correct Attorney:

SUSAN

When I initially started my divorce, I chose my attorney based on a recommendation. Once we started working on my divorce, I found that there wasn't a lot of communication between us. As the settlement unfolded and the Divorce Agreement was written, there were a lot of things that I wasn't sure of. I reached out to my attorney a lot, but he didn't return my phone calls. I really struggled with the lack of communication because it was so scary not knowing what was to come. We completed my Divorce Agreement, but I felt rushed and signed it without a complete understanding, even though I requested explanations. The explanations I did receive from my attorney were short, with a clear air of annoyance in his tone, which intimidated me. It turned out that after my divorce was final, the agreement required modifications because of important items that my attorney did not include in the original agreement. I had to hire a second attorney to look over the agreement. The second attorney was better with communication, but I felt that he didn't give me the time that I really needed or deserved. I eventually met another attorney and my experience was completely different. She heard me.

She explained things to me. She was patient with me. She was compassionate, which is something that you really need when you're going through the court system. It can be a very frightening time, full of uncertainties and confusion.

So, it really is important to find a person who can help guide you through the process. It can be very intimidating and there are a lot of things that you don't realize and don't understand, and you need someone who is going to take the time and hear you and hold your hand through the process. It's not easy to find, but it's worth taking the time and really making the effort to consult with multiple attorneys until you feel that you have found someone that you're comfortable with.

RICK

The first lawyer I retained was a disaster. The final straw came in the early stages of the divorce. Some paperwork needed to be attended to, and after weeks of not hearing a word, I called the office. They told me that the paralegal who was working on my file had quit some weeks earlier and nobody had been assigned to my case since. AND they billed me for that phone call. So, they charged me to tell me that they were NOT working on my case. Really. As I think about it now, it's almost funny, but believe me at the time I was far from laughing.

LAWYERS, LAWYERS, LAWYERS

If you were to ask a random person what he/she thinks about attorneys, there's a good chance the response would be negative. I thought about inserting a lawyer joke here, but the jokes are all so horrible that I couldn't bring myself to do it. Unfortunately, there are so many bad lawyers that an endless amount of jokes have been made about us. There are tons of horrible lawyer jokes for a reason. Even Shakespeare famously wrote in *Henry VI, Part 2, Act IV, Scene 2*, "The first thing we do, let's kill all the lawyers". So it's no secret that there are people who are not happy with lawyers.

Fortunately, there are more good lawyers than bad ones. I started this chapter with a positive quote about lawyers because what the quote says is accurate. If you hire the right lawyer for your situation, she/he will smooth out your difficulties, relieve your stress, correct mistakes, take up your burdens, and make your life more peaceful. So how do you, on your D.J., find the right lawyer for you? Like everything else in life, this will require steadfast effort and diligence. The time and effort you put in will be well worth it.

HOW TO CHOOSE

The best way to find a divorce attorney is through a word-of-mouth recommendation from someone who had a positive experience with their divorce attorney. Talk to your friends, co-workers, or family members who had a divorce attorney they liked or a family attorney they trust, who could recommend a divorce attorney for you. A referral from someone you trust will enable you to find out information about the attorney and learn what an experience with this attorney will be like before you even meet the attorney. It is usually best if someone you know and trust can tell you about the attorney's character, how they are in court, and their successes. However, nothing is foolproof as you can see from what Susan had to say. She had a word-of-mouth recommendation, and it still was not the best choice for her.

If you don't know someone who can provide a recommendation, or if you prefer to keep things private and are concerned about information being shared with your spouse, you can contact your local Bar Association. Here is a link for all of the Bar Associations in the United States: https://generalbar.com/State.aspx. When you call the Bar Association, request three recommendations for an experienced family law/divorce attorney.

Many people prefer to do an internet search since it is private, quick, and convenient. If you decide to do an internet search, you must *read the reviews* for the attorney. Reviews are usually pretty accurate. If most of the reviews about the attorney are positive and one or two are negative, then you should check the attorney out for yourself, despite the negative reviews.

If you do not have the money to hire an attorney, you can contact the legal aid program in your area. The link for all legal aid programs in the United States is: https://www.ncsc.org/topics/legal-services/legal-aid-pro-bono/resource-guide. If you qualify for legal aid based on the guidelines for the divorce court in your location, an attorney will be appointed for you. Be aware that most legal aid programs will only appoint an attorney for you in a divorce matter for issues concerning the children or domestic violence.

No matter how you choose an attorney, it is important that you meet in person to determine whether the fit is right for you prior to making the decision to hire. Your relationship with your divorce attorney is like a marriage (no pun intended), or any other relationship. Trust in the attorney and a level of comfort are necessary ingredients for the relationship to be successful.

In choosing the right lawyer, being aware of some of the reasons why people have been unhappy with their attorneys is helpful. There are many reasons, of course, and we will discuss the most common ones.

There's a television game show called *Family Feud*™ that I always think about whenever I am asked the question about choosing a lawyer. If you are not familiar with *Family Feud*™, the premise of the game is that there are two families competing against each other. They are asked questions about common topics, the answers to which were provided through surveying 100 people. The top answers are on a hidden board. One representative from each family steps up to a podium to answer a question. After the family representative gives the host the answer to the question, the game show host *says "Top three answers on the board - survey says..."* and then the answers are turned over on the board. During my over 25 years of practice, I have had many occasions where I represented a client who had previously been represented by another lawyer and was dissatisfied with that lawyer prior to hiring me to continue with their divorce. Whenever the client tells me the reason for switching attorneys, it's usually some variation of the same three reasons. And I always hear in my head: -*"Top three answers on the board-survey says:"*

1   *The attorney did not return my phone calls*
2. *The attorney did not listen to me*
3. *The attorney did not stand up for me in court*

The "top three answers" that I listed above are a big deal when you're in court for your divorce. It cannot be overstated that the attorney you choose for your divorce will affect every aspect of your divorce. This is why you should interview multiple lawyers and be aware of what to look for and what to avoid. When you speak with the attorney's office for the first time, pay attention. At www.radnalaw.com/YGDNW/forms/LawyerPhoneChecklist, you will find a checklist of what to look for when you first contact the attorney on the phone. Have this form in front of you when you call. You should print out a separate sheet for each attorney that you call. In addition to the name and contact information for the attorney, you will find the following list of things on the LAWYER PHONE CHECKLIST to pay attention to when you telephone a potential attorney:

1. How did the person whom you spoke with treat you?
2. Were they polite?
3. Were they kind?
4. Did they pay attention to what you said?
5. Did they explain clearly what the fee arrangement would be?

If the answer to more than two of those questions is "NO", contact the next attorney's office.

Once the meeting is scheduled, prepare for it. Always remember, you are going to this meeting to see if this attorney is the right person to help you through your divorce. You're not just finding out if they are nice and friendly. You also want to get a feel for whether they are knowledgeable about the issues in your divorce and the only way to do this is to discuss your issues with them and see what their responses are. But, in order to discuss your issues, *you have to prepare*. To make sure that you don't forget anything, it is best to write down (or type) your notes. Use the form that I created for this purpose which can be found at www.radnalaw. com/YGDNW/forms/LawyerConsultPrep. This form will help you to organize your thoughts and be prepared for your meeting with your potential divorce lawyer. On the LAWYER CONSULT PREP© form, you will write down:

1. How many children you have
2. Your income
3. Your spouse's income
4. Whether you own your home
5. The current value of the house
6. The amount of the mortgage remaining on the house
7. The amount of any debt accumulated during the marriage
8. With whom the children will live
9. Which spouse will remain in the marital residence

10. A list of any assets of the marriage including businesses, real estate, cars, boats, jewelry, retirement accounts and brokerage accounts
11. Any issues that you are having concerning abuse, neglect, substance abuse, mental illness, or domestic violence
12. Whether you have a pre-nuptial or post-nuptial agreement
13. Any other issues
14. Any emergencies that must be addressed

Any emergency such as domestic violence, abuse, neglect, substance abuse, mental illness, or an immediate financial situation should be discussed first. In the case of an emergency, you should bring documentation such as police reports or court orders to the attorney's office at the first meeting. If there is not an emergency situation, this is not necessary, so don't worry about bringing financial documents concerning your assets or income to the first consultation. The goal of your first meeting with a potential divorce attorney is to see how the attorney answers your questions, what plan he/she comes up with for you and whether you feel comfortable with him/her. To take some of the guesswork out of the meeting, go to: www.radnalaw.com/YGDNW/forms/ConsultChecklist. The CONSULT CHECKLIST© consists of two parts. Part one of the CONSULT CHECKLIST© contains the questions you should ask the attorney and should be used during the consultation. Part two of the CONSULT CHECKLIST© is for you to use after the meeting. In addition to the name and contact information for the attorney and her/his law firm, Part one of the CONSULT CHECKLIST© form contains the following:

1. Discuss your issues.
2. What is the attorney or the firm's communication process?
3. Will the attorney with whom you are meeting be the person whom you will be working with throughout your divorce?
4. Who else in the firm will be working with you on your divorce?

5. Will you have the opportunity to review letters or court documents before they are sent to your spouse's attorney or filed with the court?
6. Will you receive your own copy of the papers filed throughout your divorce?
7. What is the attorney's advice about how you should proceed?
8. Any other questions you would like to ask.
9. What are the attorney's fees?
10. Are you expected to pay with a retainer in advance or something else?

Each of the above questions is discussed in detail below.

YOUR ISSUES

At the consultation with your potential divorce attorney, you will be discussing the issues that are involved in your divorce. These issues are important to you. They involve your life and what your life will be A.D. (After Divorce). A good potential divorce attorney should let you tell your story with minimal interruption. Any interruptions should consist of questions to better understand or clarify something that you said. You should not be made to feel rushed or that what you're saying is unimportant. If you're organized (and you will be because you filled out your LAWYER CONSULT PREP© form) you will be able to explain your issues clearly to the attorney. After you finish telling the attorney what your issues are, you should be given advice about how the attorney and the court would likely handle your issues. The point of the consultation is for you to evaluate the attorney's approach to the issues that you present.

Be aware that if the attorney rushes you and does not seem to have time to listen to you during that initial meeting, it is likely that you will experience the same behaviour throughout your attorney client relationship. The attorney that you choose to represent you should be knowledgeable about the issues that you discuss. The attorney should seem confident and be kind when listening to you. You should be able to tell that you are being heard. The attorney should not be checking a phone or be distracted and doing other things during the meeting. When the attorney responds to your questions, ask yourself:

1. Are the answers sensible?
2. Is this someone that you will be proud to have represent you in court?
3. Does the attorney appear to be knowledgeable about the court system in your area?
4. Is the attorney knowledgeable about the issues involved in your divorce?
5. Were explanations clear and understandable?
6. Did you feel comfortable?

The goal of the interview is to have "YES" answers to the preceding six questions. Again, if you have more than two "NO" answers, move on to the next attorney on your list until you find the right fit.

COMMUNICATION

The relationship with your divorce attorney, especially if your divorce is going through the court system, is different from other attorney-client relationships. If you have an attorney who is representing you for a real estate matter, personal injury matter or business matter, you may not have to communicate with him/her very often. The attorney will speak with you initially and then speak with you periodically as the matter progresses. If any of those cases are in court, often the client is not required to appear in court with the attorney. Divorce court is different. A divorce case deals with issues that are very personal and often urgent. Therefore, *the availability of your attorney for communication is crucial.*

For example, if you have an issue concerning one of your children, like you find out that your spouse has stopped paying child support or spousal support, or canceled your credit cards or withdrew all the money from the bank accounts, these urgent situations will require immediate attention. If you can't get in touch with your attorney by phone, email, text message or some other method, how will you receive help? You require the advice of your attorney on how to proceed on virtually everything that happens during your divorce court matter. So, clearly, communication is important, and it should be discussed at your initial consultation. You should make sure to inquire about your potential divorce attorney's communication process. Even if you understand that your divorce attorney may have other divorce matters that they are handling, your divorce is currently the most important matter in your life. It's important for the lawyer to have a system in place to respond to you when you reach out.

During your consultation, ask what the attorney's communication process is. Will the attorney's mobile phone number be provided to you for contact during off hours or emergencies? If the attorney is not available, will someone else in the office return your call and address your issue? Will you be permitted to contact the attorney by email or text message? What is the response time for the firm when you call? Will the attorney return your call within 24 hours?

These are important questions. If you call your attorney about an urgent matter and you don't hear back for three days, or not at all, it may be too late, and your divorce court matter may be negatively affected. *Do not skip the communication process discussion.*

ARE YOU MY LAWYER?

A common complaint about divorce lawyers is that at the initial consultation the client met with one attorney, but then never spoke with that attorney again. After the initial meeting, when calling the office, the client was handed off to a paralegal or legal assistant or a different attorney who was unfamiliar with the facts of the divorce. When the client went to court and was expecting the original attorney, a different attorney, who was not familiar with the issues appeared and the client felt poorly represented.

To prevent a similar situation in your divorce court matter, ask the attorney at the initial consultation who will attend court appearances with you and with whom you will be speaking when you have a question. It's fine if there are other attorneys in the firm working on your divorce, but you should know this in advance. If the attorney tells you that there will be other attorneys working on your divorce, *ask to meet those attorneys*. If there are paralegals who are going to be working on your divorce, ask to meet them as well. If you're hiring a firm with multiple attorneys and support staff, you have the right to know who will be working on your divorce. It will make your relationship with the firm better and prevent unrealistic expectations.

INVOLVED IN THE PROCESS

For the best possible result concerning your divorce, you should be involved in the process. That means that any letters written, or documents filed with the court requesting any type of remedy or relief should be reviewed by you before it is sent to your spouse's attorney or finalized and sent to the court. That is because the facts in a divorce case are fluid. They are always changing. You may have initially contacted your attorney and requested a letter to be written to your spouse's attorney concerning an unpaid expense that your spouse was responsible to pay. Then, by the time the letter was written, your spouse made a partial payment so the amount due to you differed from what you originally told your attorney. Maybe when you told your attorney about an incident, you did not have information that was completely accurate. If you have the opportunity to review the letter or court document prior to it being sent to your spouse's attorney or filed with the court, you will be able to correct anything that is inaccurate. If you do not have the opportunity to review the letter, it may be sent to your spouse's attorney with incorrect facts, which may diminish your credibility-- and your spouse's lawyer may attempt to use that against you in the future. If incorrect documents are filed with the court, you may not obtain what you requested from the court or your divorce may be negatively impacted in other ways. For these reasons, it is very important that you ask the attorney at the initial consultation whether you will be provided with copies of letters in your divorce before they are finalized and sent to the court or your spouse's attorney. Ask if you will be given the opportunity to review all documents that are being submitted to the court before they are filed and if you will receive your own copy of all letters and court filings in your case. Most divorce attorneys provide these items by email throughout the divorce.

THE PLAN

At the close of the consultation, after you have provided the attorney the information about the issues involved in your divorce, *you should be given a general plan* of how the attorney would proceed if retained. This does not have to be a detailed plan, but the attorney should be able to advise you of a proposed plan. For example, would the attorney address your issues by contacting your spouse's attorney or filing papers with court? You could ask the attorney if there are any alternatives to the suggested plan or if there any other ways that your situation could be handled. If the attorney suggests a plan that you think makes sense, that may be a compelling reason for you to hire that attorney. Listening to your potential attorney's plan for your divorce is a crucial part of your consultation.

PAYMENT

It is also important to know how you will pay your attorney. Does the attorney expect a retainer in advance, meaning that a fee will be collected for a certain number of hours prior to starting to work on your divorce? What is the attorney's hourly rate? How often will you be billed for services? Is payment expected by check, credit card or some other method? Those are all questions that you should have the answers to before you decide to hire your attorney.

After you meet with the potential attorney, review, and complete part two of the CONSULT CHECKLIST© form. The items on the Part two of the CONSULT CHECKLIST© are:

1. How were you greeted by the staff or the attorney when you came to the office?
2. Were they professional?
3. Did the office seem organized?
4. Did the attorney rush you while you were explaining your situation?
5. Did the attorney interrupt you repeatedly when you were explaining your situation?
6. Did the attorney appear to be knowledgeable about the issues that you discussed?
7. Did the attorney appear to be confident?
8. Did the attorney have a plan for you by the end of the meeting?
9. Did the attorney clearly explain the firm's communication process?

10. Was the billing and payment process explained clearly and in detail?

You should interview as many attorneys as is necessary for you to find one that "checks all the boxes". After interviewing the attorneys, you will find one that you feel comfortable with and that you believe has the confidence, compassion, and ability to help you in your situation. When you do, you have found the correct attorney.

WORKING WITH YOUR ATTORNEY

Now that you have chosen your attorney, the work begins. You will give your attorney all of the required information to advocate for you during your divorce. You will be working together towards your goals for your A.D. life. *Your relationship with your attorney is a partnership.* Your attorney will only know what your issues are and what your current situation is if you tell him/her. Your attorney will only be able to prove your issues if you give him/her the evidence. That means that you must do your part, just like your attorney must do his/her part.

JENNIFER

> *Being diligent about keeping my documentation is definitely something that I learned to stay on top of. When I had a situation, I gathered my information and gave that information to my attorney who would then decide what needed to be put forth to the court, in order to get a court order in place to protect my children. Having an attorney that understands and has compassion, especially in a situation where there is abuse, addictive personalities or substance abuse, is very helpful. It can be very intimidating, frightening, and stressful,*

so having an attorney who is patient with you, understands your situation and really wants to go the extra mile to help protect your children, is very important. I learned that there was no room for fear. I had to be ready to use the resources that were available to me. When I had proof that my children were in harm's way because of something that my ex-husband did, I called child protective services. I learned not to be afraid to make that phone call to get the extra protection that they needed. Even when the judge on my case told me that I had to "get child protective services off speed dial" when I went to court with my attorney to get protection for my children from their father. Luckily, I had an attorney that kept explaining to me that if I had proof that my children were in harm's way, there was never a time that I shouldn't call child protective services. That's what they're there for. My attorney and I worked together on everything. I gave her a problem and she found a solution. I was always in the loop. That same judge later awarded everything that we requested. My children were protected and are doing so well now.

If there is an issue that arises which requires your attorney's assistance, you should ask your attorney what you must provide in order to be successful in obtaining the relief that you are requesting. Once the attorney tells you what you must provide, do your part and get it done as soon as possible. You should review anything the attorney sends you right away so that any requested changes may be made quickly and deadlines will be met. The attorney can only help you if you do your part. If there is a court order, you should follow it. If there is a reason why you cannot follow the court order, you must let your attorney know immediately. Your attorney is there to give you the advice necessary to complete your D.J. successfully. If you follow your attorney's advice and are diligent about providing the requested information, you are giving yourself the best chance to obtain your desired outcome.

CHAPTER 3

DOLLARS AND SENSE

"*Divorce is one of the most financially traumatic things you can go through.*"

- Richard Wagner

DORIS

I was foolish enough to believe that the $5,000 retainer would pay for the whole divorce. I was wrong. I ended up using the money that I had saved in order to move on with my life after the divorce to pay for the attorneys, because it was just so much more expensive.

JEAN

I was very surprised at the cost of an attorney. I had not set aside money and needed help from my family. The attorney charged by the hour and as time went on it caused me a great deal of stress waiting around in court all day.

People are always shocked by the amount of money that is spent on a divorce. It almost always seems like no matter how much you save, or how much you are prepared to pay, you end up spending more, especially if the divorce is contested[6].

The best analogy I can think of is Disneyland™, believe it or not. You know the drill. You research the cost of the vacation, you plan for the costs of the airfare, rental car, hotel, and amusement park. You set aside spending money, you pack all of the right clothes, you even get the coupons and discounts. But in the end, you still spend more than what you prepared for. And it's the little things. Like T-shirts and food and unexpected items like raincoats and socks that increase the bill. The bill ends up being a number that was completely different, and much higher, than what you anticipated. And that's what it's like when you get divorced. The total amount that will ultimately be spent on legal fees to your divorce attorney will be based on how much time and effort is required to reach a final agreement, which makes the final amount paid unpredictable. Remember, your attorney cannot force your spouse to agree, and reaching a final agreement may require more time and effort than you expect.

---

[6] A divorce is considered "contested" if you and your spouse do not agree on most issues.

ATTORNEY FEES

For contested divorces, most divorce attorneys charge by the hour. Divorce attorneys usually require an initial retainer, which is a payment, in advance, that is a multiple of their hourly rate. In other words, they may require a retainer for 10 hours, 20 hours, or 30 hours of work in advance to start working on your divorce. The formula to calculate an attorney's retainer fee is:

Hourly Rate (\$) multiplied by Number of Hours (#) = Total Retainer Fee (\$\$)

In the United States, the hourly rate for a divorce attorney can range anywhere from less than \$150 per hour to more than \$1000 per hour, depending on where you live in the country. Let's use an example of an hourly rate of \$500 per hour. If the lawyer required a 10-hour retainer, the total retainer fee would be \$5,000. If the lawyer required a 20-hour retainer, the total retainer fee would be \$10,000. The initial retainer is not necessarily the entire cost of the divorce. Recall what Doris said at the beginning of this chapter. If there is a great deal of work to be done in your divorce, that retainer will be required to be replenished, meaning more money must be added to it. This will occur as the attorney working on your divorce uses up the time you paid for with the original retainer.

The retainer fees can really add up. If your divorce is contested, you will be going to court. The attorney who goes to court with you must prepare for court, appear at court and then do work on your divorce matter after court. You will be charged for all of that before, during and after time. There may be slight variations throughout the country on how attorneys charge in a divorce, but that is generally how it works. And you can imagine how all of those hours add up to be a large bill over time.

OTHER COSTS

After accounting for the cost of your attorney, you must also anticipate court costs, investigative and appraisal costs and possibly attorney costs for your children. A list of some fees that you may incur are:[7]

1. **FILING FEES:** To file, or start, your divorce, most states charge a filing fee. Also, if you file a motion[8], most states require a motion filing fee.

2. **PROCESS SERVER FEES:** Your spouse is usually required to be served[9] personally with the divorce papers. Professional process servers charge a fee.

3. **SUBPOENA FEES:** If documents must be subpoenaed during the course of your divorce, there is a fee associated with doing so.

4. **COURT REPORTER FEES:** Court proceedings are recorded by a court reporter. At times, it may be necessary for you to obtain the transcript[10] for the court proceeding. The court reporter charges a fee to produce the transcript.

5. **FORENSIC ACCOUNTANT FEES:** If you or your spouse own a business that is a marital asset, your attorney retains a forensic accountant to determine the value of

---

[7] This is a list of some of the common extra fees that you may pay and does not include every possible fee that you may incur in addition to your attorney fees.

[8] A motion is a request to the court for some type of relief such as temporary custody, child support or spousal support while your divorce is pending. Motions may also be made during and after your divorce to enforce a court order.

[9] To be "served" in the context of a divorce or a lawsuit is to have court papers delivered to someone in person.

[10] A transcript is the word for word typewritten recording of everything that was said during your court appearance.

the business. Additionally, a forensic accountant can be utilized to investigate money that you believe your spouse has hidden. You are responsible for those fees.

6. **FEES FOR THE ATTORNEY FOR THE CHILDREN:** In certain instances, when there are issues involving custody, visitation or safety of the children, the court will appoint an attorney for the children. There may be a cost for that attorney which you and your spouse would be responsible for.

7. **HOUSE APPRAISAL FEES:** There could be a cost for the appraisal of your house.

This is not a comprehensive list. There may be other costs. The point is: divorces that are addressed and litigated in court are expensive.

LIFE, INTERRUPTED

MATT

The cost of my divorce was substantial because it was a contested divorce. Even the simplest step involved letters back and forth, and that's a bill. Also, the stress of the divorce made me feel like my head wasn't really in the game a lot of the time. I own a business, but I felt like I wasn't 100% mentally there, so my business slipped quite a bit. And because of everything that was happening with my divorce, sometimes I was just like "whatever" about the business. It was almost like an out of body experience. I almost looked at it like it was someone else's life. And I just went through the motions. It affected me financially. I had to go into my savings. Thank God I had savings, but that was significantly cut into. My wife also did

***stuff to sabotage my business, so that hurt my business too.
I had to cancel patients because of court appearances that I
was required to attend. Even if court wasn't the entire day, it
was hard to go back to work for the rest of the day because I
just wasn't emotionally there after going to court.***

Your life is interrupted when you are going through your divorce;
both emotionally and financially. As you heard from Matt, if you
own your own business, the requirements of everything that must
be done for the divorce will periodically take you away from your
business. You have paperwork to prepare, meetings to attend with
your attorney, and court appearances where you are required to
be present. If you are employed, you are put in the position of
asking your employer for permission to take the day off to go
to court. All of those things affect your ability to work and may
affect your income. So now you have something that's expensive
(your divorce) and you have your income being affected by the
divorce. If you own your own business, you may not be able to
pay the same attention to it as usual which may reduce the amount
of your referrals, which may in turn affect your income. If your
children are young, you may be doing everything that is required
for your divorce after you put them to bed at night, making you
feel constantly tired. Hang in there; you will get through this. I'm
just giving you full disclosure.

THE PLAN

A plan helps you to control the financial cost of your divorce. First,
you should have a goal as to what you would like to accomplish
in your divorce. You made an initial plan in Chapter 1 when you
filled out the INITIAL PLAN© form found at www.radnalaw.
com/YGDNW/forms/InitialPlan. Now it's time for that plan to
become more detailed. By filling in the details and determining
what issues you and your spouse agree about and which ones you

do not agree about, you narrow the issues that must be submitted to the judge for decision. By narrowing the issues, you save money.

Again, this falls into a few categories: marital residence, children, and division of marital assets. Although that sounds a lot simpler than it actually is. At www.radnalaw.com/YGDNW/forms/ InterimPlan, you can print out the sheet that will help you with your INTERIM PLAN©. The form contains the categories we just listed. The categories are discussed in detail below.

MARITAL RESIDENCE

GEORGE

After I made the decision to get divorced, I also made the decision to stay in the house with my soon to be ex-wife throughout the divorce process. I was the more nurturing parent, and a better caretaker than my wife was. I needed to be there for my children. However, that environment was toxic. It was terrible. Yes, it was important for me to be there for my children, but because I was there, they saw the horrible arguments that my ex-wife and I got into. Shit that was said back and forth. I would do the best I could to avoid any confrontation with my ex, but sometimes I would just see red because of things that she did or said. My wife and I had been together for over two decades. She knew exactly which buttons to push and how to get me going. It was bad. What the court finally did, since neither one of us was willing to move out of the house, which sounds insane to say out loud now, but at the time it seemed reasonable, was that we had assigned nights at the house. We had assigned weekends where every other weekend one of us would have to leave from Friday to Sunday. We also had assigned nights during the week which was our time with our daughters. When it wasn't our night, we were supposed to make ourselves scarce, which my wife did not always do. Sometimes there would be a confrontation. It was just nuts. If my daughters came to talk to me on my wife's night, even if it was just for minute, my wife would be screaming "Not your night!" It was crazy! I would pretend that I didn't hear her and kept talking to my daughter like everything was fine. I started staying at work as late as possible so that I wouldn't be in the house on my wife's night. I had planned to stay in the house until our divorce was final or at least until the Divorce Agreement was signed, but I moved out sooner than that. Staying there was too hard on me and too hard on our children because of the constant fighting. I got my own place and my daughters visited me there. It was so much more peaceful and enjoyable.

Deciding who will stay in the marital residence, sometimes is an easy decision agreed upon between spouses, but not always. The house that you lived in during your marriage has a lot of emotions attached to it. It's perhaps where you raised your children. You invested time and money into the house. Once you decide to get divorced you next must decide if that house still makes sense for you. Can you still afford it on just one income? Do you need all the room that you have in that house? Although it may seem that those are questions to be considered for your A.D. (After Divorce) life, you should also decide if you should stay in the house *during* the divorce. George just told you what it was like for him when he decided to stay in the house during the divorce. The answer for you will be based on your circumstances. If you and your spouse are able to keep the arguments to a minimum, it might make sense for you to stay in the house so the children have both of you in the same place, until you at least have a written and signed Divorce Agreement. If possible, this option may be beneficial, especially if you have young children. If there's a lot of arguing between you and your spouse, both of you staying in the house together is not the best choice for your children. Learn from George's experience and don't subject your children to the arguments between you and your spouse. It affects the children, and the goal is to get your children through this divorce with minimal distress.

Maybe you both remaining in the house until the divorce is final is for financial reasons. If that's the case, think of ways to make both of you living in the house while you're going through the divorce easier. Maybe each of you can stay in different sections of the house or, if possible, different rooms or floors in the house.

If your spouse has falsely accused you of physical abuse in the past, be aware that if you stay in the house those accusations will continue and may place you in a dangerous situation.

Those are all things that you should discuss with your attorney when determining what makes sense for you in your particular circumstances. There are no easy answers in a divorce. Every decision that you make has a consequence. Who stays in the house and who leaves should be one of the first things that you think through and must be part of your INTERIM PLAN©. If there is not an agreement about the house, then that will be an issue to be addressed in court and on your INTERIM PLAN© you should write the words NO AGREEMENT-DECIDE IN COURT.

THE BUYOUT

If both you and your spouse are owners of the house, when you reach an agreement, the person who is staying in the house will have to pay the person who is moving out of the house for his/her share of the equity in the house. If your name is not on the deed/ title of the house, your divorce attorney will advise as to whether you are considered an owner of the house you lived in during the marriage. Write down on your INTERIM PLAN© the current value of your house. If you don't know, look at real estate listings

43

for houses in your neighborhood that are similar to your house to get a general idea. If you have a mortgage on your house, look at your most recent mortgage statement and write the outstanding balance on your INTERIM PLAN©.

The formula to calculate the equity in your house is:

$$\text{Value of House } (V) \text{ minus Mortgage Balance } (M) =$$
$$\text{Equity in the house } (E)$$

If you and your spouse are equal owners of the house, the person who remains in the house will pay the person who leaves 50% of the equity. There are different ways to work this out, and your lawyer will advise you about this issue. The takeaway here is that you should know whether you and your spouse are able to agree about who will remain in the house, whether the person who is choosing to remain in the house can afford to pay the monthly bills and buy out the person who is leaving, or whether the marital residence is an issue that requires the court's assistance.

CHILDREN

If you and your spouse have children, this is the next category to be completed on your INTERIM PLAN© form. If you and your spouse do not have children, skip this section and go to the marital assets section. If you do have children, go to the CHILDREN section on your INTERIM PLAN© form. If custody of the children is not agreed-upon, and an agreement cannot be worked out during the course of your divorce, then this is something that will have to be decided in court. Write on the form for this section NO AGREEMENT-DECIDE IN COURT. If it is agreed-upon, then who will be the primary custodial parent[11] is not something that

---

[11] The primary custodial parent is the parent that the child will live with for the majority of the week.

must be decided in court. However, you still must discuss visitation/parenting time. Your attorney will guide you through the details of a visitation/access/parenting time schedule for the other parent and this will all ultimately become part of your Divorce Agreement.

DIVISION OF MARITAL ASSETS

The INTERIM PLAN© form provides space for you to list all the assets you have accumulated during the marriage and everything that you believe you should each be receiving a percentage of. You have already put most of these items in the list on your INITIAL PLAN© form. This form is designed to be more detailed. You can copy and paste the items that you had on the original list onto the INTERIM PLAN© list. Next to each item, list the current financial value. This will require a little more time and research into your accounts. This exercise will give you a clearer picture of the value of the marital assets and will help to bring your A.D. life into focus.

ECONOMIC SENSE

PAUL

My wife told me that she wanted to divorce on the day after my sister's funeral. My sister had been sick with cancer for over a year. During the last months of her life, I spent a lot of time with my sister and my mother, who was losing her daughter. My wife was annoyed that I wasn't spending enough time at home with the family because I was spending time with my sister. I run my own business and I was going straight from work to help take care of my sister and relieve my mother. When my wife first told me that she wanted a divorce she said that she wanted to do a collaborative divorce. That meant that we were supposed to try to work everything out. But that *didn't happen. If I didn't agree with exactly what she wanted, then we couldn't have an agreement. It was her way or no way. But what she wanted was unreasonable. One of the most shocking things to me was how much the divorce cost. First, I had to pay the collaborative divorce attorney. Then I had to get the new attorney when we had the contested divorce. And since my wife worked part-time in my business and I made more money than she did, I had to pay the fees for her lawyer too. She fought about every single thing and made the attorneys' fees go even higher than they needed to be. She even fought about a ladder that I wanted when I was moving out of the house. She wasn't going to use it. She just fought for it because I wanted it. I probably spent $5000 in attorneys' fees fighting over that $200 ladder. It was ridiculous. I didn't want to give in to my wife because she had been so horrible throughout the divorce. I'm still paying off my attorney, and I was divorced two years ago!*

To determine if it makes economic sense for you to go to court and whether you have funds available to pay for a divorce, you should know what your finances are, including income from your employment and assets. If you don't have enough funds to spend many hours in court, it would make sense for you to try to decide which battles you are going to fight and which ones you may decide to cut your losses on. Your attorney should be instrumental in helping you to assess what is worth fighting over and what is not. The ladder that Paul just told us he spent $5,000 in lawyer's fees fighting over only cost $200. That is just one example. Throughout your divorce, issues will arise that will force you to decide whether to litigate in court or agree to something different from what you originally wanted to save time and money. There are some issues where the decision will be clear. For example, an emergency issue involving your safety or the safety of your children. But other situations may not be as clear. This is where the partnership and good communication with your attorney is crucial. You should be able to have the economic sense discussion with your attorney with regard to any issue that you are considering litigating in court.

CHAPTER 4

WE MAY HAVE TO LITIGATE

"Everyone is right from their perspective."

\- Bob Proctor

In a perfect world you and your spouse would agree about everything, put it all in your Divorce Agreement, and have an easy-peasy, uneventful, amicable divorce. Unfortunately, that's not everyone's situation. There are many very good reasons why people may require a judge to decide an issue in their divorce. Not everyone has an agreeable spouse who just says, "Sure, whatever you want". You will know if you have to litigate and go to court by the discussions or arguments you have with your spouse. If your spouse argues with you about everything, refuses to listen to reason, or thinks he/she is always right and you are always wrong, you will likely have to go to court. Sometimes you have to go to court because it's an emergency, other times it's for another issue such as custody, child support, spousal support, visitation, division of marital assets or any other divorce-related issue that you and your spouse cannot agree upon. This can happen even if, from your perspective, you feel that your requests are reasonable. Eileen (see below) had an emergency situation that required her to go to court. Here's what happened:

EILEEN

> *My husband was very controlling throughout our marriage. He was from a different country. He wanted our child to have dual citizenship. I agreed. She was an American citizen, but she was also a citizen of my husband's country. My husband constantly threatened that he was going to take our daughter to his country so that I wouldn't see her. She was only two years old. I knew that he had connections there. I was concerned that the threat was real. During one difficult argument with him, he threatened again to take her and leave, and I was highly concerned that he would act on the threat. I called the police. Then I called an attorney. The attorney filed papers in court, and I was able to get a court order that prevented him from leaving the country with our daughter. The court even kept our daughter's passport so that my husband couldn't leave the country with her unless there was a court order. I felt safer as soon as that court order was in place.*

Not every situation is like Eileen's. When it's an emergency, it's clear that you have to go to court. But sometimes it's not so clear. Sometimes you feel that you should just be able to work it out, or your spouse might have told you that he/she would work it out but for some reason it drags on and there's been no solution. Court will help to move things along and keep your spouse accountable.

ANTHONY

After 26 years of marriage, my wife told me that she wanted a divorce. I was blown away. I had worked all these years. She was a stay-at-home mom. I was very involved in the lives of my sons. I thought everything was fine between us. I thought we were a happy family. We had friends together. But I was wrong. My wife told me that she wanted to go to mediation, so I agreed. And then when I went to see the mediator, he told me that he was representing my wife and not me. From that point on, the divorce became contested. My wife would not agree to anything, even when I told her that I would give her half of everything and we could share the visitation with the kids. No. Instead it was a complete war. We fought about everything, through our attorneys. Getting to an agreement was really, really tough. Going to court and having the pressure of an upcoming trial date is what ultimately led us to complete the Divorce Agreement. I'm so glad it's over.

Most people do not want to go to court for their divorce. It is preferable for it to be resolved without a judge being involved. Even though you are in court, your attorney should always be working on resolving the case. Your attorney will do this by speaking with you, your spouse's attorney, and with the court, if necessary, until an agreement is reached. Although the preference is to come to a quick agreement, that's not what always happens. Sometimes you must go to court. But how do you know if your situation calls for that? You might think of yourself as a very reasonable, agreeable person. However, it takes two people to have an agreement. Like the quote at the beginning of this chapter says, "Everyone is right from their perspective." You may think that whatever it is that you are requesting is very reasonable, and your spouse may believe that the reason for his/her objection to your request is very reasonable as well. If the two of you are unable to reach an agreement about an important issue, court is your alternative and your solution to get the issue decided and resolved.

So, what's the purpose of court? What can court do that you can't get done by just trying to talk it out with your spouse? While you may not be able to persuade your spouse to see things your way and you may feel that your spouse is stringing you along, once a judge is assigned to your divorce, you and your spouse will both be held accountable. The judge can put orders into place that must be followed by both husband and wife. For example, the judge can issue orders concerning custody, child support, spousal support, visitation/parenting time, supervised visitation, drug testing, and the list goes on. Once those orders are issued, they must be followed to avoid penalties.

AL

My divorce was contested. Every little thing was an issue. Just to give an example, the visitation part of it took time to hammer out. There were drafts of the agreement going back and forth and since my wife and I had different thoughts about particular matters, that had to be negotiated and renegotiated, until it was finally done. Then at the next court date around a month later, she wanted to change it. That's how it went. On every issue. The judge gave us deadlines for when we had to complete things, and it was the accountability caused by the court orders and deadlines that finally got us to a settlement.

Sometimes a decision about whether you must go to court is simply based on the fact that you cannot agree on anything no matter how hard you try. That was Al's situation. You cannot force someone to agree. If you and your attorneys are trying to work out an agreement with your spouse and weeks turn into months or even years without an agreement, the best way for you to get results is to go to court. Sometimes simply having the judge telling both you and your spouse exactly what the law is and explaining "here's what's going to happen if you go forward with the trial" might be exactly what the doctor ordered for your divorce to be finally resolved. If not, then you go to trial, and that's how it will be finished. At a minimum, going to court will help you chip away at the issues in your divorce. Court will add gravity and urgency to the situation. In other words, once you're in court, your spouse will know that this is serious and that you both have to get everything done by a deadline set by the court. That usually makes things start moving so you don't feel that your divorce is stagnant.

Sometimes your spouse promises to come to an agreement wth you, but instead keeps "kicking the can down the road and saying, "I'll get back to you next week" or "I'll get back to you in a couple weeks" or "I just was busy with work and I'll get to it as soon as possible" or " I am meeting with my attorney next week to go over your proposal". It could be dozens of excuses. But, at the end of the day, you want to get on with your life and you want to get these things resolved, so court might be your best option.

As long as you go to court prepared with your attorney, who should be advocating for your best interests, everything will eventually work out. Court will feel intimidating at first, but as long as everyone pays attention to detail and clearly conveys the issues, it usually ends up getting resolved. It might not be resolved in the way that you initially envisioned it would be, but it will get resolved.

CHAPTER 5

THE JUDGE

"Here comes the Judge."

- Pigmeat Markham

The judge plays a very important role in the outcome of your divorce. The reason that you are in court is because you and your spouse were unable to agree about some, or all, of the issues involved in your divorce. You are in court to ask the judge to make those decisions. You are therefore putting a lot of faith in the judge. The judge will decide issues that will be affecting your life for years. The judge will decide issues about your children, your finances, and your A.D. (After Divorce) life. This is something for which you must be prepared.

By now you should have formulated your plan of what you want your A.D. life to look like. You have chosen your attorney, and you are aware of the issues on which you and your spouse agree or disagree.

You are likely also wondering what the actual experience with the judge will be like. Will the judge see that you are a good person who just wants a fair deal in your divorce? Will the judge be interested in the fact that you are an involved parent who coaches your child's sport teams or volunteers at his school's Parent Association? Will the judge respect that you are a pillar of your community and you work hard at your job, or that you have built your own business against the odds? These are all good questions. The short answer is that everything about you as a parent, spouse, and financial provider, as well as your good character is analyzed and scrutinized. However, the judge may not give your good attributes the weight that you expect. To illustrate these points, read what some of your FDWs (Fellow Divorce Warriors) have to say.

BOB

> *What surprised me was that the judge ultimately doesn't care about you. It's like you were the asshole who let your marriage go bad and this is why you're here. And it's not that the judge was saying "this is your punishment", but it's kind of like "this is the bed you made and now you gotta lie in it and deal with it". So, they really couldn't give a shit about you. They do care about the kids. The adults in the relationship, that's a different story. It's like I'm screaming "my head's on fire" and they're saying "there's a bathroom downstairs, take the stairs, you'll find it, stick your head in the toilet. You'll be ok." That's the feeling that I got about how the judge felt about us as adults. For the kids, however, the world came to a screeching halt. Which at the time, I kind of agreed with the judge. I was like ok, yeah. But it was surprising. Not what I expected.*

Many of my clients have told me that before going to court, they expected that the judge would care that they were involved in the children's school, that people in the community thought they were a good person, that they were very involved in their children's lives throughout the entire marriage, or whatever other attributes that they felt made them a nice, decent, and good person. The reality is that the judge analyzes your whole situation without emotion. To the judge, your marriage is simply a contractual agreement. Now that the contractual relationship has come to an end, the judge's role in the process is to facilitate a fair outcome for the parties to the marriage contract and to ensure the safety of the children. It does not matter how famous, rich, or poor you are. To the judge, everyone should be on an even playing field. The numbers may be different as far as marital assets and child support, but the goals in every divorce are basically the same. Even though that sounds very fair and reasonable, the reality is that when you are in court, the judges may seem to be abrupt, uncaring, and critical. Remember, it is not personal. They do not have anything against you. They are just doing their job. Here is what Ashley and Nadia had to say about their experiences in court:

ASHLEY

Over the years, because of various issues, I went to court many times with different judges. I remember crying a lot when I would go to court because of the way the judges spoke to me. There are certain things that they have less tolerance for. Even something as small as saying "my children" instead of "our children" would result in some type of lecture from the judge. I remember just feeling that I really had to prove myself over and over again. Even after the first few times when I felt that I had established credibility with the judge, there were some days that I walked in and felt that I had to do it all over again. It's very, very frustrating to have to do that. But you have to remain strong, and you have to continue to do that until you achieve your goals.

NADIA

> *You have to have a thick skin when the judge speaks to you in a certain way, which may come across as disrespectful. It is hard not to be emotional, and it's ok if you are. There are many times that I cried. Some judges were patient with it, and some were not. Take it from me, you have every right to take your time and pull yourself together. There were times when I just could not get the words out. I was so nervous that I wasn't going to be able to say what I knew the judge needed to hear. At the end of the day, the judge will give you the time to do that. You can turn to your attorney and say that you need a minute or just wait until you are able to get your point across without crying. If you have all of the right information and the right documentation, you will be heard.*

At this point in your D.J. (Divorce Journey), it is important for you to know what to expect from the judge, and what the judge expects from you. When your divorce is being decided in court, you will see the judge a number of times. Your attorney will address the different issues that you are having with your spouse. There are conferences where your attorney will speak to the judge on your behalf. Sometimes the judge will question you directly about the issues involved in your divorce in the presence of your attorney. Here are some rules to remember for when you speak with the judge and for when the judge is speaking in general:

1. **Be respectful.** Address the Judge as "Your Honor" or "Judge".

2. **No interruptions.** When you are in court and the judge is speaking, you should never interrupt. Let the judge finish what she/he is saying.

3. **Poker face.** Do not make faces, gestures, sounds or anything to exhibit your displeasure with what the judge is saying. If the judge is not speaking to you directly, wait for your attorney to speak on your behalf.

4. **Wait for it.** Only speak to the judge if the judge addresses you directly and/or gives you permission to speak.

5. **Your spouse's turn.** When your spouse is speaking do not interrupt if the judge is speaking with him/her.

6. **Make eye contact.** Look at the judge and listen to what he/she is saying. You should not be looking at your phone or at your feet or appear that you are not paying attention.

7. **Answer the question.** If the judge has asked you a question, you should answer respectfully. Do not go into a whole long story. Answer the question that the judge is asking you. If there is additional information that you want to add that the judge did not ask you about, ask the judge for permission to speak.

8. **Respect.** Every judge will be a little different. Some judges may be less formal than others. But every judge expects respect and if you are respectful, they are more likely to listen to you.

9. **You are in a fishbowl.** The judge evaluates your credibility and demeanor each time that you appear before him/her.

10. **No bickering.** The judge does not want to hear your negative comments about your spouse, so think to yourself.

Be aware that the judge who is assigned to your divorce is also presiding over many other divorces. The issues that they hear at times may be emergencies while other issues may be more routine. Due to large caseloads assigned to the judges, it is very important for you and your attorney to be organized with a clear goal of what you wish to achieve at each court appearance.

You may feel when you go to court that the judge did not spend that much time with you, or that the judge may have been short with you when you were speaking, or that the judge did not give you a chance to say what you wanted to say. Resolving your issues through divorce court is a long game, not a short one. Your attorney's role is to advocate for you and ensure that the judge is aware of the facts and circumstances from your perspective as well as your spouse's. Although it may not be apparent on your first day in court, if you follow the suggestions in this book, are organized, have given your attorney the information they require in order to advocate for you, and have chosen an attorney who is a strong advocate on your behalf, your attorney will be able to convey all of the important information that the judge requires to make a fair decision.

In a contested divorce, you will see the judge many times. If your claim is valid and your attorney is clearly and strongly presenting your case, eventually the judge will learn what the true situation is.

CHAPTER 6

READY, SET, GO

"Before anything else, preparation is the key to success."
- Alexander Graham Bell

If you decide that court is necessary, you must be prepared and have a clear understanding of what it is that you want to accomplish. Every court appearance is your attorney's chance to present you in the best light to achieve your goal. Everything you want to tell a judge and why the judge should decide in your favor must be proven with evidence. Evidence is your words supported by documentation. Proof of your claim gives you credibility and increases your chances of success.

JEAN

> *I learned early on that bringing documentation with me to court gave me credibility with the judge. Going back and forth with my ex-husband didn't help my case. My ex-husband made horrible accusations against me, but he never had documentation. Having accurate documentation, whether it was e-mails, text messages, phone records, police reports, or court transcripts really made the difference in proving my case and being successful concerning the many issues that my attorney and I brought to court.*

COURT PREP

Your goals in divorce court usually fall into two categories: your children or your money. To be prepared for court, you should be clear about why you are going to court. To help you prepare, go to: www.radnalaw.com/YGDNW/forms/CourtPrep, and print out the COURT PREP© form. On the form, you will see the words "issue", "concerns" and "proof". Next to the word "issue", identify the issues, stating why you are going to court. For example, if the issue is your children, you are going to write "children" next to the word "issue". If the issue is child support or spousal support, write those words down next to the word "issue". Underneath the word "issue" you will see the word "concerns". On the lines underneath the word "concerns" write down all of the concerns that you have about the issue. Those are the concerns that you would like the court to address and determine.

CHILDREN

Issues involving the children usually fall into the categories of custody, visitation, or child support. In the category of custody, you may wish the court to issue a custody order if you do not yet have one. Write on your COURT PREP© form the reasons why you believe there should be a custody order appointing you as the primary custodial parent. Your attorney will speak with the court on your behalf, but you must provide your attorney with the information to adequately be your advocate and your voice in court. Your COURT PREP© form will help you identify the reasons why you believe you should have custody and gather the proof that supports your reasons. With the proof, your attorney will be able to make legal arguments for why the court should award you custody. The items on your COURT PREP© form do not have to be complicated. They could be as simple as stating that you are the parent with the schedule that allows you to spend more time with the children, get them to and from school, and help them with their homework, to cite a few examples. The courts will determine what is in the best interest of your children, based on the arguments your attorney makes with the proof that you provide.

If you have serious concerns about your children, such as your spouse abusing alcohol or drugs or being under the influence while with the children, you must be able to prove those allegations. The court does not decide based on suspicions. You should always have proof of your suspicions. Other examples may be situations like these: you picked up the children from your spouse/former spouse and the children told you that they had not eaten because their father/mother had been sleeping all day and there was no food in the house. Or you smelled alcohol on your spouse/former spouse's breath when he/she drove the children to your home after parenting time with them.

If the children were in a dangerous situation, such as the other parent driving while under the influence, you should call the child protective service agency in your area or the police. [12] However,

---

[12] For the police call 911. For child protective services agencies in the United States, go to https://www.childwelfare.gov/organizations.

many times there's a fine line that separates a situation that's dangerous and one that's cause for concern. You should not call the police unless you have a legitimate reason to do so. Witnessing your child's other parent driving under the influence, for example, would be a legitimate reason to contact the police.

If your concern is that your children are being abused, either verbally or physically, you should call Child Protective Services. [13]

Sometimes the issues are not as drastic as abuse or neglect. They could be simply that your children's other parent is claiming that you are not making the children available for parenting time or visitation. If it is your position that you have made the children available, but the children's other parent always cancels the visitation, the best way to be able to prove your position is through emails and text messages. For example, if your child's other parent is supposed to visit the children every other weekend, and you have text messages that state that the he/she actually canceled visitation, that would be helpful evidence. In your COURT PREP© form, notate under "proof" the words "text" or "email".

TRACKING EXPENSES

If the issue is about child support and your claim is that your child's other parent is not paying the court-ordered "extra expenses of the child", then you should have receipts, proof of payment and the original plus the copies of the invoices requesting the payment. I have heard the complaint that "it is too complicated to keep track of all of the expenses. If you know how to make a spreadsheet and have access to a computer and a scanner, that is ideal. Simply track all of the items that you spend money on for your children on the

---

[13] https://www.childwelfare.gov/organizations. After clicking on the link choose "State Child Abuse Reporting Numbers" for the phone number of the agency in your area.

spreadsheet and scan the receipts, invoices, and proof of payment into your computer for possible future use.

However, if you're not familiar with spreadsheets and scanners, tracking the expenses does not require a high-tech format. A simple low-tech way to keep track of the expenses is to purchase manila envelopes and label them. They could be labeled "lunch expenses", "dance expenses" "medical payments", etc. Then use the expense tracker found at: www.radnalaw.com/YGDNW/forms/OutOfPocketExpenseTracker, and print out the OUT OF POCKET EXPENSE TRACKER© form. Print out a separate form for each expense. For example, one for dance expenses, one for medical expenses, etc. It is not necessary to have a spreadsheet. Then look at the receipts and invoices in your manila envelopes for each category of your expenses once a month. Write out the expense, date of the invoice, date paid, and the date that you requested a payment from your spouse for their share of the expenses. A simple listing of what the expenses are is fine as long as it is clear, dated and organized.

COMMUNICATION WITH YOUR SPOUSE

If you have a contentious relationship with your spouse, the best way to protect yourself against baseless accusations is to limit all communications to email and text messages. By doing so, you will have documentation of all of your conversations. If your spouse claims that you, for example, withheld your children from visitation, through your text messages you will be able to prove that the children were available, and it was actually your spouse who canceled the visitation. If it was in a text message, you have it in writing and it will be a lot easier to prove than if it is just your word against your spouse's.

FINANCES

If you want to prove anything about the finances, you should have tax returns, pay stubs, bank statements, receipts, or credit card statements to prove your financial claims. If you want to prove the amount of your spouse's income, for example, you should have copies of W-2s, tax returns and paystubs, or any other proof that shows what his/her income is. Credit card debt or expenses can be proven through credit card statements, etc.

THE CHECKLIST

Once you have completed your COURT PREP© list, speak to your attorney about what to expect at the court appearance. At www.radnalaw.com/YGDNW/forms/CourtQuestions you can print out the COURT QUESTIONS© form, which has a list of suggested questions that you may ask your attorney prior to your court appearance. You may add other questions for your attorney as well. The point is, you want to feel ready before you go to court. This is true for every court appearance that you will have throughout your D.J. (Divorce Journey). Fear and anxiety are most often due to the unknown. Even though there is no way to predict exactly what the outcome of your court appearance will be, knowledge about the process and what your plan is should diminish the fear and anxiety that you are experiencing.

Questions to ask your attorney before your first court appearance can include:

1. Do I have to be present?
2. What will happen at the first court date?
3. If I am required to be present, what is the name of the judge and what do you know about how the judge handles my type of case?

4. What papers should I bring with me to court?
5. Can I have a copy of any papers that were filed with the court on my behalf?
6. What is the goal of the court appearance?
7. Which attorney from the firm will be meeting me at court?
8. Where should we meet and at what time?

Once you have the answers to the questions on the COURT QUESTIONS© checklist and after you gather the items that your attorney advised you to have, schedule an in-person meeting with your attorney to go over what is expected to occur in court. Knowledge is power and it will make you feel in control as you go into the unknown of your first court appearance.

CHAPTER 7

YOUR DAY IN COURT

"If you only knew."

- Shinedown

Court is the first time that anyone besides your family, friends and attorneys are going to hear your story. There is often a great deal of fear and anxiety associated with going to court for your divorce, especially the first time. Even though you have been planning to go to court with your attorney, when the day finally comes, it's nerve-racking. It's the fear of the unknown. An extremely important point to highlight is that you may think you know what to expect, and then you may find out what actually happens is completely different from what you expected. This chapter will help you to understand what to expect. Knowing what to expect will reduce some of the fear and anxiety. FDWs (Fellow Divorce Warriors) Stephanie, Joe and Kim share their experiences below:

STEPHANIE

Court is a scary place whether you're a felon or whether you're just trying to get divorced. Nobody cares about the way you feel. Nobody tries to smooth or soften the process. It's like a meat market, and the judge just tries to rush you in and out of the room. They ask a few quick questions to the attorneys. You don't get to say anything. You're just a number. You're a nobody. Then they rush you out and you already paid for, let's say four hours of your attorney's time, so you feel like you've gotten nowhere, and you spent $2,000.00 for the morning. It's horrible.

JOE

I remember the judge calling us up because it was our first day. He said something like "Your lives, as a marriage is ending, but you'll always be parents". He talked about how important that is and you have to get through this and do the right thing for them. I remember him saying "You both are still pillars of their lives and they're seeing those pillars of their lives separating." He talked about how trying that is for them. Before the judge said that, I never really looked at it that way. I remember it being very upsetting and choking back tears. It was awful.

KIM

When I was going to court for the first time about my divorce, I remember feeling confident that the judge would understand what I had gone through with my husband since he was a drug addict and there were children involved. I was confident because I knew what kind of parent I was and what kind of person I was. I was sure that it wouldn't be an issue upon meeting the judge. But that wasn't what happened. The court looks at everyone on the same level. Even if, in my eyes, I did the right thing and my husband was doing the wrong thing, the court looked at us both the same in the beginning. At that time, I remember that I felt like a criminal because of how I was treated and the way that I was spoken to. I could sense the impatience from the judge when she spoke to me, which was very intimidating and upsetting. I had to prove myself and everything that I wanted the judge to know, despite the dismissive way the judge seemed to act.

I know that what Stephanie, Joe, and Kim just told you is intimidating. But what they said is true. The judges in divorce courts see so many cases that you are, in a sense, just another divorce to them. They listen and analyze what you have to say without emotion. To the judges and the court, your marriage was a contract and they are just overseeing the dissolution of that marital partnership. I am giving you this difficult truth so that you do not have unrealistic expectations of what court will be. Whether you are wealthy or someone of modest means, the court treats everyone the same.

Before you go to your first court appearance, ideally you would have met with your attorney and discussed what is expected to happen. Every court venue, courtroom, and judge has its own set of rules and procedures. In some courthouses, the attorneys may meet with the judge and you may not meet with the judge yourself. In other situations, the judge will address you at each court appearance in open court with a court reporter transcribing all discussions. Some judges may require you to be present at every court appearance, while other judges may excuse you from being present. Your attorney should be able to advise you of the rules and procedures of your particular court venue and judge prior to the first appearance.

At the first court appearance, you should dress neatly. You should get to the courthouse early. Many times, there's a security line to get through and you don't want the court officer to call your case while you're not at the courtroom yet because you're outside in line. Make sure you know where the courthouse is located so that you don't get lost that day on the way there. If you are not sure of the location or how to get there, take a practice drive prior to your first court date. Leave yourself plenty of time to get there. Make sure that you know specifically where you are meeting your attorney so that you can find him/her when you get to the courthouse.

It is fine if you bring someone with you to court for support, but she/he may not be permitted to enter the courtroom with you. You should check with your attorney about who you may bring with you to court. The new girlfriend or boyfriend might not be a good person to bring to court if that person was one of the factors in the breakup of your marriage. It's not that you're hiding who you're with now, it's just that you're trying to keep emotions down when you're in court. You're also trying to see what positive outcomes you can work towards in your divorce. Bringing somebody else to divorce court who is likely to make emotions run high may interfere with achieving your objectives for that court appearance.

You should not bring your teenaged or older children with you to court for support. The judge does not like to see children being involved in the court case in any way, including just bringing them to court for moral support. That is because children, even adult children, should not be made to "take sides" in your divorce. Even if your opinion is that your child is angry with your spouse and is more aligned with you, the court will hold it against you if there is a perception that you have played a role in the child having these feelings or opinions. If the child comes to court with you, it gives the appearance that you are encouraging your child to align himself/herself against your spouse. The court will likely take note of that, which may impact you negatively when the judge decides the issues involved in your divorce.

If you have young children and you don't have someone to take care of them while you are in court, you should discuss that issue with your attorney prior to your court date. There should be someone to take care of the children and they should not be in court with you, if possible. Some courthouses have provisions for daycare for young children while you are in court. Your attorney should be able to provide you with that information.

Many people bring their parents to court with them. That is fine, but you should have an understanding with your parents about whether you want them to be involved in negotiations. The negotiations should really be between you, your spouse, and your attorneys. While your parents can be there for moral support, it sometimes makes things more difficult if they are trying to insert themselves into negotiations. Especially if they have a different perspective on things than you do. Even if your parents are helping you financially, you should discuss with them how you want things to proceed. At the end of the day, this is your situation, and the discussion about your parents' role in your divorce is something that should take place before you go to court. Your attorney should also be aware of what your parents' role is. Your attorney should know whether your parents will be present during your attorney-client discussions or whether you will just let them know what is going on after a private discussion with your attorney.

In most courthouses throughout the country, divorce court is a crowded place. In rural areas, it may be less crowded. In most courthouses there are court officers, other people who are getting divorced, attorneys, judges and court attorneys who work with the judges. That's a lot of people. You may feel overwhelmed when you see all the people there. The people that you see at the courthouse are there because they have some type of issue that cannot be resolved, and they need the court to help. Your case is just as important as anyone else's. You will get your turn. Remember that and be patient. Go to court expecting that you will have to wait. If you had to take the day off from work, expect to be there for the day and be pleasantly surprised if you finish early. If you expect to be there for the day, you will be less anxious while you are waiting. It is very stressful if you have an appointment on the same day as your court appearances. It may cause you to worry about being on time for your appointment instead of thinking about the issues in your divorce.

Once you get to court, your attorney should meet with you before you see the judge. Your attorney should explain what is expected to happen (hopefully for at least the second time, since you met prior to the day of the court appearance). After all that is done, you wait for your case to be called.

WHAT ACTUALLY HAPPENS

If it is the first court appearance and it was not an emergency, the judge will usually ask your attorney and your spouse's attorney what the circumstances surrounding your divorce are and what issues are currently unresolved. The judge will ask if the parties are able to settle.

Your attorney will usually speak with the other attorney while you are in court to determine if you are able to work out a settlement. This is important. You should know what it is that you are willing to do to settle. So, what does it mean to "settle"? You know what it is that you wanted to achieve. You know why you went to court in the first place. But there may be some things that you're willing to give up in order to resolve the case, save on future attorneys' fees, and not have to be in court repeatedly, for a long period of time. When both parties give something up and meet in the middle, that's a settlement.

Divorces can stretch out to weeks, months, or years. Only you will know what it is that you're willing to negotiate and what is non-negotiable. You can only get to that point by speaking with your attorney, who will be familiar with what your spouse's attorney is relating. This is why the relationship with your attorney is so important. Again, make sure that you have given your attorney all the proof of any of the claims that you're making. If you submitted papers before you went to court, all the proof should be attached to those papers. You will usually feel a little calmer if you have a copy of those papers yourself and your attorney does not have the only copy. Don't forget to ask your attorney for a copy of the papers *before* you go to court.

When your attorney is speaking with you about the divorce or trying to negotiate a settlement, remember what your goals are. You wrote them down on your INITIAL PLAN© form, your INTERIM PLAN© form and your COURT PREP© form. Remember to pay attention while you are in court because the attorney might not remember all the details. For example, a detail may be that an appointment was scheduled for when your child is going to be away on some type of school event. Or it might be that your child has an important doctor's appointment on a date that something is going to be scheduled. Your attorney will not know that unless you tell him/her. That's why you must keep talking to your attorney. Pay attention to dates. Have your calendar with you for when future court dates or attorney appointments are scheduled. If you wish to discuss visitation between your child and your spouse, have the child's schedule with you so that available dates and times may be arranged.

If there are going to be discussions about money, you should know what your expenses are, what you are and are not willing to negotiate. If you have particular monthly expenses and no other source of income, it doesn't make sense to agree to accept an amount lower than what you need in order to pay your bills.

At the same time, it will not help you to negotiate for a higher number just to prove a point. Negotiate an amount that you feel is fair and sufficient, not punitive.

While it is important for your attorney to communicate with you, you must also communicate with your attorney. The attorney is not going to know what it is that you need in your particular situation if you don't tell him/her. A successful court date is based on a partnership between you and your attorney. You should provide your attorney with all the background and current information regarding your needs so that she/he can articulately and legally convey those needs to the judge when you are in court.

At every court appearance there should be a goal of what's going to be accomplished. Ask your attorney what the purpose is of this court appearance. What is supposed to be happening on this date?

When you're in court, if the judge is speaking to you while you are with your attorney, you should respond to the judge, but you should not interrupt the judge. Be respectful and address the judge as "Your Honor" or "Judge".

After you appear before the judge, your attorney should explain to you what happened. Even though you were in the courtroom and even if the judge spoke to you directly, sometimes it's a little overwhelming. It's new for you, but it's not new for your attorney. There are things that the attorney will understand about what happened that you may not understand. The attorney should also let you know what your next steps are. If the attorney doesn't volunteer this information, you should ask her/him to explain to you what happened and what the next steps are. You should know when your next court date is and what you have to do prior to that date. If there's paperwork that must be filed, your attorney should explain what must be filed and when it is due. It will usually take more than one court appearance to resolve all of your issues. Once you understand what you are required to do or provide prior to the next court date, schedule a date to meet with your attorney to discuss all issues.

EMERGENCIES

If you're in court for an emergency, you should have read the papers that your attorney submitted before you go to court. In some situations, those papers would have been signed by you, and in other situations they would have been signed solely by your lawyer. Before your court appearance, ask your attorney for a copy of the papers so you understand what it is that you are asking the court for. Before you go to court ask your attorney what is supposed to be happening in court on that day, so you understand.

If you were supposed to have a hearing at that first court appearance because it was an emergency, you should have prepared with your attorney for that hearing. A successful court appearance depends on your preparation before court.

You should know whether the court appearance[14] is a hearing[15] or a conference[16] or a trial[17]. If it's a hearing or trial, you should meet with your attorney to go over what will be happening. Your attorney should prepare by reviewing the questions that you are likely to be asked and reviewing the evidence that you will be providing to the court to prove your position.

A full trial does not usually occur at the first court appearance, but there may be a hearing at the first court appearance if it's for

[14] A court appearance is any time that you go to court and meet with the judge.

[15] A hearing is when the court hears testimony from witnesses and accepts evidence about limited issue in your divorce.

[16] A conference is a meeting with the attorneys and the court about the status of your divorce and the ability to resolve your issues.

[17] A trial is when the court hears testimony from witnesses and accepts evidence about all of the issues in your divorce.

some type of an emergency proceeding. Your attorney will let you know whether you will have to testify at the hearing. If it is a conference, your attorney will let you know whether you will be required to speak. Sometimes at the first court appearance, the judge will speak with you and tell you what his/her role is and what he/she expects of you. Remember, when the judge speaks, listen without interruption even if you don't like what the judge is saying. When the judge is finished speaking, your attorney will let you know if you may respond. The attorney will usually respond on your behalf, but if you would like to add something to what your attorney said, you will usually be permitted to do so.

OTHER COURT APPEARANCES

As long as you find the right attorney to advocate on your behalf, the judge will eventually be familiar with the facts of your divorce, even if in the beginning you might have felt that the judge was against you, or not listening, or didn't seem to care. At some of your court appearances, the judge will issue an order. This could be an order about paying spousal support or child support or about who must move out of the marital residence. Whatever the court order is, it must be followed. You must do exactly what the court orders direct. If your spouse does not follow the court order, remind him/her that they have to do what the court order says and if they do not, you will return to court to report the violation and ask the court for a remedy. That's the way that the court works effectively. But remember that the court order is a two-way street. You both must abide by what it directs. When you go to court to complain about your spouse's violation of a court order, the court will examine not only your spouse's actions, but your actions as well. If you have both violated the court order, the judge will take note of that.

The court order is meant to be used as a shield and not a sword. It is not meant to be used to "get back at" your spouse. Judges do not like to be involved in the vindictiveness of spouses during a divorce. If, in the judge's view, you are attempting to use the court system to vindictively hurt your spouse, that's not necessarily going to work in your favor. For example, the judge would likely look unfavorably on you if you withheld parenting time or visitation from your spouse or former spouse for failure to pay his/her share of an extracurricular activity. Your best practice is to always follow the court order and document when your spouse does not follow the court order. You will be able to bring up the violation of the court order in court and if it is solely your spouse who is repeatedly violating the court order while you are consistently adhering to it, the court will eventually see that and rule in your favor.

You will become familiar with the process as you continue to go to court. You will not be as intimidated by the judge. Getting prepared will be more understandable to you. Read what your FDWs Al and Mary experienced in court:

AL

As you continue to go to court throughout your divorce case, you're not quite as nervous. You still don't know what to expect. That's what you learn too. As much as you think you know what to expect, you actually don't know what to expect. It's not as scary anymore. It's still scary in that it's your life that's hanging in the balance. But you're not losing sleep about an upcoming court date. You almost get used to it. You know the procedure. You don't get quite as nervous when the lawyers go in the back to speak to the judge. You still don't know what's going to have been accomplished at the end of that court appearance. But you get used to the process, the steps, the faces of everyone involved. It becomes more procedural than this emotional, scary, frightening, experience. The judge gets to know what everyone's position is and you

start to see things moving forward, even though it may still take, at least in my case, a very long time until everything is done and you're actually divorced.

MARY

It's not easy, but in the end, you will never feel the judge taking a side. They'll never show their cards that way. But you have to feel confident in your documentation, in the things that you're saying, that the judge will hear you. One of my issues was that my ex was very vocal in the courtroom and he would interrupt and speak more. I was worried that because he was not afraid to be vocal, he would be heard better than I was. But in the end, that didn't turn out to be the case. He said everything he wanted to say, but he couldn't back it up with any proof. I had to be confident that the judge would eventually see that, and she did. It is very upsetting and frustrating that you know who you are and what you are, but that doesn't necessarily come across once you walk into a courtroom. You just have to hang in there even though it's a very difficult and painful situation. In my situation, whenever we were in court, the courtroom was full of other attorneys and other people waiting to have their cases heard by the judge. It's very intimidating to be in that situation knowing all eyes are on you when you're trying to state your case. You just have to breathe and take your time and get your point across. You're better off not being too vocal and maybe just listening a little bit more and taking time before you speak rather than just shooting from the hip. That can really make a difference at the end of the day.

If you have clear goals and proof of your claims when you go to court, eventually the judge will rule fairly. The trick is that when you go to court, you must remember that the judge is not going to decide based on emotion. They are going to decide based on the law. In deciding to bring an issue to the court, remove your emotions and then analyze your situation to see if the issue is one for the judge to decide. For example, if you are going to court to request that primary custody should be changed from your spouse to you, the basis for the request should not be your anger because your spouse did not bring your children to your grandmother's birthday party on your spouse's parenting day. That would be the emotional side of it. If instead you request custody since it is in the best interest of your children as your spouse is not able to care for them due to their work schedule, that would be an argument based on the law.

Whether you are going to court concerning an issue with the children, for financial support, or division of marital assets, you should be prepared to prove your position. The judge will not rule in your favor if you are unable to prove your claims.

THE DIVORCE AGREEMENT

KATE

> *One of the things that I felt was frustrating with my first attorney was that my Divorce Agreement was too standard. My situation in my divorce required a little more attention due to the fact that my ex-husband was a drug addict. There were protective measures that were overlooked as far as our children were concerned. One of the things that I remember changing was their visitation with their father in the summertime – the attorney put in the Divorce Agreement that my ex-husband would have two straight weeks and then one additional week for three weeks of summer vacation with our children. This eventually had to change because for them to be in his care for that period of time was not safe for our children. The frustrating part for me was that my attorney and I worked on*

81

the stipulation outside of court, so it could have been tailored to the things that were going to be the safest measures for our children, and it wasn't. We had that opportunity and the time to do that, but I felt that it was just put together quickly and overlooked a lot of very important protective factors for the kids. The agreement was costly. I had to go to court to have things modified to make it a safer environment for our children when they visited their father. When we were putting my agreement together, I felt pressured. I felt that my attorney was frustrated; wanted to get it over with. I really didn't fully understand the contents of every section of the agreement and I regretted that in the end. I really should have made him take the time to sit down with me and really make sure that I understood everything that was written. There could have been things that saved me future trips to court and financial worries that could have been avoided in the beginning. He kept telling me that the court was going to award my ex-husband a lot of the things in the Agreement anyway so it would be in my best interest to just sign it and that turned out not to be the case, so that was very frustrating to me.

MADELINE

I had a really tough time getting through my divorce with my husband. My husband alienated my daughter against me. It was shocking. My daughter was an adult and she still believed the lies that my husband told about me. But I got through it all. I dealt with it. As part of the divorce I was supposed to get 50% of my husband's retirement account. We were married for over 20 years. It was fair. I trusted my attorney. Years later when I knew that my husband was retired, because he was much older than I was, I was wondering why I didn't get the retirement money. I consulted with my new attorney. When she went through my agreement, although it generally said that we would each receive 50% of the retirement accounts, it didn't list the names that the accounts were in, or the name of the pension plan, or the address of the institutions that held the accounts. The agreement also did not indicate the amount of money that was in each account at the time that we signed the divorce agreement. In addition, my former attorney never obtained the court order that was required to divide the accounts once I was divorced. I no longer had a current address for my ex-husband. We just couldn't find him. I was just without that money. After spending all that money on lawyer fees to get that divorce agreement. I wish I knew that my agreement had to be specific. Nobody told me. We went to court to try to get the agreement enforced, but the way that it was written, there was very little the court was able to do. Shocking! Horrible! Everyone should know the importance of a specific divorce agreement. Don't be bullied by your attorney or anyone else into signing an agreement before you fully understand it. Learn from what happened to me and make sure that your agreement is specific.

SPECIFICS, SPECIFICS, SPECIFICS

The goal of divorce court is to come to an agreement one way or the other. That agreement may be reached after going to court a number of times, or it might come at the end of a trial when you get a decision. In either situation, you're going to end up with the Judgment of Divorce and either a decision from the court after trial, or from an agreement between you and your spouse. Your Judgment of Divorce and Divorce Agreement are binding contracts that you will live by after your divorce. Therefore, it is very important for the agreement or the court order to be very specific. It is difficult to enforce something that is too general, as we heard from Madeline. It's easier for the court to enforce an agreement that is specific. For example, the visitation schedule for the children should include holidays. The holiday schedule should list all of the holidays and indicate who will have parenting time with the children in each year, with times of day for each parent specified. If the agreement generally indicates that you and your spouse will share the holidays 50-50, it will be difficult for the judge to rule that you should have a specific holiday, for example, Christmas, instead of your spouse since the agreement is so general. But, if your agreement states that you have Christmas in even years starting at 12:00 p.m., that is clearly enforceable.

If you have children, your divorce agreement should indicate who is the primary custodial parent that the children will live with the majority of the time. There should be a visitation schedule that is specific.

The agreement should clearly address the division of marital assets. It should specifically list each marital asset and specify which assets each spouse will be receiving. If you are dividing household furniture, there should be a schedule attached to your agreement listing all the furniture that each one of you will be taking. If, for example, you are being "bought out" of the marital residence and both of your names are on the mortgage and the deed, the agreement should specify the date when you will be paid for your share of the equity in the house, the date the deed will be changed to your spouse's name and the date by which your name will be removed from the mortgage. If there are debts of the marriage that are required to be paid, the agreement should specifically state what must be paid, by whom and by what date.

The point is that the agreement should specifically state everything that you agreed to, in detail, in order for it to be enforceable. Make sure that you understand what is in your agreement. Go over it with your attorney. You should go through every single section of your Divorce Agreement with your attorney in his/her office and make sure that you understand it before you sign it. The judge will assume that since you signed the agreement, you agreed to it. It is very difficult to change the agreement after it has been signed by both you and your spouse. *Do not agree to sign the agreement in court if you have not thoroughly reviewed it with your attorney prior to your court date.* This is why communication with your attorney is very important. You must know what's happening at every court appearance. If you have already reviewed the agreement and you have agreed to sign it in court after your review, that would be acceptable. However, if you're reviewing it for the first time in court, there will be a great deal of time pressure on you. You may not have time to think through everything, and you may not have time to make sure that it is exactly what you wish to have in your Divorce Agreement. This is the most important document to come out of your divorce. You are going to be living with it for a long time. Make sure it is correct and contains everything that you require.

CHAPTER 8

WHEN YOUR SPOUSE OR FORMER SPOUSE ABUSES SUBSTANCES OR HAS MENTAL ILLNESS

"Addiction affects all members of the household in different ways."
- Healthline.com

Alcohol, drugs, and mental illness are horrible issues to deal with under any circumstances. They can be a nightmare that is even more terrifying and complicated during a divorce with children involved. It is worse in a divorce because when you were together during the marriage, you were there to make sure that things would stay under control. Often while you are in a marriage with someone who has mental illness or abuses substances, you handle whatever the issues are because when not under the influence, or when the mental illness is controlled by prescribed medicines, the person you love is pleasant, kind and responsible and everything is fine. It's a different story, as you know, when he/she is off of their meds or under the influence. When you are divorced or going through a divorce and living in separate places, the children are seeing their other parent without you present, which may be dangerous.

The courts will help you to navigate the very difficult circumstance of having a spouse with mental illness or substance abuse issues. Through court orders, the court can direct treatment in the case of mental illness or substance abuse, require testing in the case of substance abuse, and order a change of custody and/or supervised visitation when necessary. These are potentially scary situations that your attorney and the courts are able to guide you through so that you and your children will feel safe and protected. Here is what some of your FDWs experienced with these issues:

MENTAL ILLNESS

NEIL

My wife was addicted to drugs and had mental illness. No matter how much I spoke to her, she continued to use illicit drugs to self-medicate. I would think that everything was okay and then I would come home and find out that she was asleep on the couch and the baby was playing by himself on the floor. One day I got a call that my wife was in the hospital with the children because she couldn't remember if the baby took the pills that she left open unintentionally. That was very scary. The baby ended up being okay, but it was too close for comfort. I called a lawyer. The lawyer took us to court and got a court order that allowed my wife to only be with our children if I was there or somebody else was supervising her until she got her mental illness under control.

Leaving your children in the care of a parent with uncontrolled mental illness is a potentially dangerous situation. If your spouse has mental illness that is not controlled with medication, it is very important that at the beginning of your divorce you bring an emergency petition in court to either obtain an order of protection or supervised visitation so that your children will be safe. The procedural steps that must be undertaken to achieve those objectives will vary from state to state. Your attorney will help you through the process. Remember that you will be required to prove every single thing that you are claiming. If the issue is mental illness, you will be required to provide proof of your spouse's behavior or psychiatric hospitalizations. If the issue is substance abuse, you should be prepared to provide proof of your spouse being under the influence while with the children.

MARIE

My son's father had mental illness. He did not have a diagnosis, but after we separated, he would send me long, rambling text messages. He would tell me that he hated me and that he didn't want to see our son, then he would say that he wanted us to be together, then he would say that he wanted custody of our son. His messages were, abusive, threatening, and nonstop. Because of his mental illness it was impossible to get him to listen to reason. I hired an attorney. We went to court and got court orders for him to have a mental health evaluation and had an attorney appointed for our son. In the end, the court ordered supervised visitation for him, but it was a long, scary road. Our son is seven years old now and is happy and well adjusted. Leaving his father was one of the best decisions I made.

When your spouse has mental illness, it is a roller coaster ride for you. Although seemingly normal and nice while taking prescribed medications, your spouse becomes unpredictable and dangerous when not controlled by medications. If your spouse has been diagnosed with mental illness, the current medical provider and therapist can be helpful in ensuring proper medications to control symptoms. If someone with mental illness is properly medicated with their behaviors under control, supervised parenting time is unnecessary. If your spouse/former spouse is not properly or adequately medicated and they are displaying frightening or aggressive behavior or appear to be incoherent and saying things that do not make sense, call 911 and their treating doctor for in-patient treatment. To protect your children and yourself, if you are still living together, bring an emergency court proceeding, with the assistance of your attorney. Give your attorney proof in the form of police reports, hospital reports and, if possible, a statement from the doctor who is treating your spouse. If you have proof of your claims, your attorney will be able to obtain the necessary court orders for you.

At times people with mental illness may attempt to self-medicate with alcohol and drugs. The result is that the symptoms associated with his/her mental illness are made worse. Sometimes a drastic behavioral change in a person, whose mental illness was controlled with medication, is because the person abruptly stopped taking medications.

If your spouse has mental illness, go to www.radnalaw.com/YGDNW/forms/Mental-Illness, and fill out the MENTAL ILLNESS© form with the following:

1. The medications that are prescribed to your spouse
2. The names and contact information of his/her medical providers

3. The names and addresses of the hospitals or in-patient psychiatric facilities as well as the dates when they were receiving in-patient care
4. Your spouse's diagnosis and how it was controlled during the marriage
5. The contact information of any witnesses to your spouse's recent disorderly or abusive behavior due to mental illness
6. Copies of any police reports concerning your spouse's mental illness
7. Any letters, emails or text messages concerning your spouse's mental illness
8. Copies of reports or findings of any child protective agencies concerning incidents of abuse or neglect where the claims concerning your spouse were found to be credible

The above information will help you to prove your case if you find it necessary to obtain protection for you and/or your children through the court.

SUBSTANCE ADDICTIONS

If your spouse/former spouse has substance addictions, you may find yourself in court many times to address the issues. Like a person with mental illness, a person who is addicted to substances[18] will have periods of sobriety and periods of active use. Going through a divorce with mental health or substance abuse issues is difficult. Obtaining the protections that you require for you and your children is time-consuming, expensive, and sometimes degrading and embarrassing. Unfortunately, no one can go through it for you. This is something that you must handle personally, with the help of your attorney and the other agencies that were created

---

[18] Substances are illicit drugs, prescription narcotics or alcohol

solely for helping people in similar situations to yours. You will get through. Read what Barbara did to protect her children:

BARBARA

As hard as it was, and I went through this for many years, your perseverance and strength are really what's going to help your children in the long run. It felt never-ending. Always having to go to court to prove myself; prove my ex's addiction. But it was worth it to protect my children as I have their entire lives. It was not easy. It was hurtful. It was expensive. It was frustrating. But I had to persevere. Every time that I felt that my children were in danger, I brought it to the court's attention. It never got easier for me to go to court. I would be physically sick the night before court due to emotional anxiety, but I knew at the end of the day if I was able to prove that my children were in danger, they would be protected and that meant everything to me. I did whatever it took to keep my children safe, even though it was frightening. At times when I went into court, the judge spoke to me at a certain level which I felt was unfair, and painful. Other times I went to court and explained that my ex-husband was using drugs again and I would have to succumb to drug testing as well, even though I have never used drugs. The drug testing was humiliating. I would have to urinate in front of a drug test employee with the door open or put my head upside down and let them cut chunks out of my hair so that they could analyze it to make sure I wasn't using drugs. I did what I needed to do at the time. It was hard. As painful as it was, every time I stepped up to prove that my ex was using, it was worth it because what would come of that was the protection for my children from my ex-husband who, while under the influence, drove with them, was abusive, and neglected their care. All of these years later, I feel that I saved their lives on some level because

I never gave up the fight to protect them. They went through so much in their young lives, but they had my unwavering support and they are happy, strong, young adults now.

If during the marriage, your spouse had a substance abuse issue, go to www.radnalaw.com/YGDNW/forms/SubstanceAbuse and complete the SUBSTANCE ABUSE© form with the following information:

1. The name and address of any rehabilitation facilities where your spouse received in-patient treatment

2. The dates of any arrests and/or convictions for driving under the influence

3. The titles of any court-mandated classes in which they were required to enroll concerning their substance abuse

4. The contact information of any witnesses to your spouse's recent disorderly or abusive behavior while under the influence

5. Copies of any police reports concerning your spouse's substance abuse

6. Any letters, emails or text messages concerning your spouse's substance abuse

7. Copies of reports or findings of any child protective agencies concerning incidents of abuse or neglect where the claims concerning your spouse were found to be credible.

The information that you gather about what occurred during the marriage will be additional proof if you make a request to the court to protect yourself or your children when a situation arises concerning abuse of substances.

DRUG TESTING

As Barbara just described, sometimes when you ask the court to perform a substance test on your children's other parent, the court may require you to undergo testing as well. You should agree. Be aware that if you requested the test, and the court directs that you both be tested, you will likely be required to pay for both tests. If you are sure that the children's other parent is abusing substances, the indignities that you endure, as Barbara just described, will be worth it if the other parent tests positive. A positive test result will likely result in a court order that directs your children's other parent to be supervised during visitation with the children.

If you have proof that your spouse/former spouse is under the influence or is abusing drugs or alcohol while with the children, you must ask the court for a substance test immediately. Preferably a hair follicle test. The hair follicle test will detect evidence of substances for 30, 60 or 90 days prior to the date of the analysis, depending on the length of the hair analyzed. The "instant test" or the urinalysis test will detect substances in the system for a much shorter period of time. A urine sample analysis may not be accurate if the person being tested is experienced in trying to trick the system. Request that all testing of your children's other parent for the presence of substances be performed through the court and not through a private laboratory over which the court does not have control. People who abuse alcohol and drugs are very clever and are often well-versed in tricking the system. Requesting court supervision of testing will help to prevent a false negative.

Ask your attorney to request that the court issue an order for random testing for substances to ensure that your children's other parent maintains sobriety. Random testing means that with very short notice, testing will be conducted for substances. If your child's other parent is abusing substances, it will be revealed. The court order will protect you. In other words, if there's a court order that directs that your children's other parent may not to be under the influence of substances when with the children and you find out that he/she was under the influence of substances in the presence of the children, you may return to court to report the violation of the court order. Your attorney will request the penalties and remedies available for you due to the violation.

BE DILIGENT

If you are not able to prove drug or alcohol use by your children's other parent before the court order for visitation goes into effect, you must be diligent. If, for example, you pick up your child after visitation at your spouse/former spouse's home and you suspect that he/she is under the influence, you should notify your attorney immediately. Your attorney will submit the necessary paperwork to court to have your spouse/former spouse tested for substances and obtain a court order for supervised visitation. If something dangerous occurs, such as your spouse/former spouse driving under the influence with the child, depending on when you find out about the dangerous behavior, you should call the police and contact Child Protective Services. The link for all of the child protective services agencies in the United States is: https://www.childwelfare.gov/organizations

If you are not able to obtain a court order for supervised visitation and your school-aged child tells you that your spouse/former spouse has been under the influence while they are together, tell your child not to get in the car with anyone who appears to be under the influence, including his/her parent. Show your child how to call 911 and get in touch with you if in a dangerous situation or if the parent is under the influence and acting in a way that is strange.

WHAT SHOULD YOU SAY TO THE KIDS?

There's a fine line between what you should and should not tell your child concerning the issues being addressed in court. There may be situations where your child may be a witness to your spouse/former spouse's behavior due to mental illness or substance abuse. The discussion that you have with your child will vary depending on his/her age. When you speak with your child about what was observed, do so in a way that does not disparage the other parent. For example, instead of saying "your father is a drug addict", or "your mother is crazy", ask the child what happened and how he/she felt. Let the child know that you will speak with the parent or that the parent may be unwell, and you will try to get some help. Reassure the child that the other parent loves them.

The number one thing is always to protect your child. Listen to what he/she is saying to you upon returning from parenting time[19] with the other parent. Let your son/daughter know that it's okay to talk to you and nobody's going to get in trouble. Children often want to protect their parent and worry that if they say something about what is occurring when they are together, they will not be able to see that parent again. Let your child know that you and your spouse/former spouse both love him/her and that you both want him/her to be safe.

If there are issues occurring and Child Protective Services or the attorney for the children scheduled time to speak with the child, explain that they are just there to help, and the child should tell the truth. Make efforts to speak with your attorney, and the attorney appointed for your child[20], and the child's therapist if he/she has

---

[19] Parental visitation is currently called "parenting time" instead of "visitation" in most states.

[20] If there has not been an attorney appointed for your children, you may request that one be appointed.

one, about the words you should use when discussing the other parent's mental health or substance abuse issues.

SAFETY NET

The role of the attorney for the children is to advocate for the children in court. To be able to do so, the attorney will meet with the children to discuss what is occurring in each parent's household. Do not tell your children what to say to their attorney. You should only tell them to explain to their attorney how they feel and to tell their attorney the truth. The attorney for the children does not represent the interests of either you or your spouse. The children may speak with their attorney outside of your presence about any issues concerning custody or visitation.

Your attorney, the attorney for the children, and child protective services, if utilized correctly, provide a safety net to protect your children if their other parent is abusing substances or has uncontrolled mental illness. Be aware that, like the court orders, the police and child protective services are meant to be used as a shield (for protection) and not a sword (for attack). If you suspect something, make sure you have proof and that your suspicions are correct before you contact any of these agencies or file a petition in court. If you repeatedly go to court or contact the police, child protective services or the attorney for the children with allegations that are proven to be untrue, that will work against you, as the judge and CPS may not believe what you claim in the future. To prove what your suspicions are to the court or the child protective agency, support your claims with text messages, e-mails, and police reports. If the proof is solely what your child observed and told you, the child will speak with his/her attorney and child protective services to explain what occurred.

THE CHILDREN'S RELATIONSHIP WITH BOTH PARENTS

The courts strive to ensure that the children have a relationship with both of their parents. The court will not disturb that unless they are given proof that the children are not safe when they are alone with one of the parents. If the court is provided with proof that the children are not safe or that the parent has a current issue of substance abuse or mental illness that is not controlled by medication, it will act to protect the children. Be aware that the fact that a parent has a history of substance abuse, or mental illness which is not currently threatening the children's safety, that history alone will likely be insufficient to obtain supervised visitation for the children. If the parent with a history of substance abuse is sober and the parent with mental illness is properly medicated and safely caring for the children, there is no reason for the court to get involved. It is only if there is a current issue that jeopardizes the safety of the children that the court will hear evidence and issue a necessary court order.

CHAPTER 9

WHAT ABOUT THE CHILDREN?

"Our children are our most precious natural resource, and there is no other way to parent but to put them first."

-Dale Archer

No matter the circumstances surrounding your divorce, the children that you have together will always have the two of you as parents. Your children love both of you. The best-case scenario is:

a. They never get put in the middle of the situations involved in your divorce
b. They have the unhampered ability, with your blessing, to love their other parent.

You may believe that your divorce is different, but the reason that I call the above your "best-case scenario" is because, my experience in divorce court is that from the perspective of the children, it often is. Despite claims that in a divorce, "children are resilient," they "bounce back," and "divorce doesn't affect them", my observations are that children of all ages are affected by the divorce. Even children as young as one to two years old show signs of anxiety and stress due to the turmoil of the divorce. From the young child's perspective, it is difficult for them to understand why one parent is no longer living with him/her and why he/she no longer sees both parents every day. Middle school children often, without verbalizing it, blame themselves for the divorce. Teenagers are often angry at one or both parents for the turmoil that the divorce has caused in their lives, and adult children often align themselves with one parent in the divorce, which may cause them to lose their relationship with the other parent.

To be fair, staying married when there are constant arguments, abuse or no apparent love and affection, also negatively affects the children. So, what should you do? Is it simply a no-win situation? The short answer is "no". But, as you can see by this point in the book, there are no easy outs. *Every good result requires effort on your part.* Again, this is not a psychology book. It's a book about what to expect when you go to court for your divorce. The fact that children are a part of the process cannot be ignored though. Your words and actions matter. Your children are watching and listening, even when you think that they are not. Your words and actions will shape them and affect the way they view you, their other parent and themselves. We all want our children to be happy, well-adjusted adults. That happy outcome depends, in large part, on you and your spouse/former spouse. If you really work on it and make a conscious effort to consider your children in the actions you take, the decisions you make and everything you say in their presence or within earshot, they will beat the odds and do well.

TELLING THE KIDS ABOUT THE DIVORCE

The first step, of course, is telling your children that their parents, are getting divorced. How you approach this first step makes all the difference. It should not be said in passing or in a moment of anger at your spouse. It also should not be heard from another family member, friend or overheard when you and your spouse are discussing it. Each of these scenarios can have a jarring effect on your children that may result in unintended repercussions. The best way to tell the children is as follows:

1. Set aside time to tell the children that you and your spouse are getting divorced. Allow enough time for the children to speak with you afterwards.

2. If possible, you and your spouse should be together when you tell the children. Alternatively, agree with your spouse to both tell them the same thing, even if you tell them separately.

3. Tell the children that you and your spouse are getting divorced. It is not necessary for you to tell the children the reason for the divorce.

4. Tell the children that you and your spouse will be living separately.

5. Tell the children that you both love them very much.

6. Explain that you will each still be spending time with them, even though you will be doing so separately.

7. Let the children know which parent will be moving out of the house and where the other parent will live.

If they know that you love them no matter the circumstances, and no matter where each of you is living, it will make the transition much easier.

THE CHILDREN ARE NOT GETTING DIVORCED, YOU ARE

Believe it or not, telling the children that you are getting divorced is the easy part. Even though you may have dreaded telling them, once you do, you're done, and you never have to do it again. When you are going through a divorce that is in court, the difficult part is making sure that you do not put the children in the middle of your issues with your spouse. Here are the things that you should not say to or in the presence of your children (you can remember this by thinking "NBC"):

1. Do not say anything **N**egative about your child's other parent.

2. Do not **B**lame the other parent for your situation.

3. Do not share with the children what is occurring in **C**ourt.[21]

Even though the list only consists of three things, I promise you that it takes discipline to implement. If you adhere to *no discussions about NBC* and are always conscious of the fact that your child loves his/her other parent (even though you are so angry at what that person is putting you through), your child's life will be less stressful.

Adhering to *no discussions about NBC* is even more difficult when your child's other parent is doing something that is jeopardizing

---

[21] There are situations where the child may be required to go to court and you absolutely should explain to them why they are going to the court in that circumstance.

your child's safety. If your spouse/former spouse has a substance-abuse issue, a mental health issue or is physically abusive, you should tell the child generally to let you know if he/she ever feels unsafe while with any adults, including a parent. As discussed earlier, your child should know how to call 911 if necessary and how to get in touch with you.

Early in your case, it is likely that the judge and your attorney will advise you that you should not discuss your court case with the child. However, if the case advances through the courts and your child is assigned an attorney, you will have to speak about the court case. Depending on the age of the child, what you say will vary. Young children should only be told what is absolutely necessary. For example, if there is a reason the child no longer wishes to go to the other parent's house and spend time there, your child's attorney will ask your child why. Tell your child that he/she has his/her own attorney and can tell the attorney how he/she feels about going to the other parent's house. Let the child know to the truth. Be aware that young children repeat everything they hear. If you tell your young child to "remember that you should tell your attorney that your mother or father…" did whatever it is that you (as the parent) wants the attorney for the child to know, it is likely that your child will tell his/her attorney "mom told me to say…" or "dad told me to say". That may make it appear to the attorney for the child that you are attempting to manipulate the child for your benefit. You should simply tell your child to tell the truth about his/her feelings when meeting with the attorney.

NO INTERROGATIONS

Teenagers become very resentful if you question them about what is happening at the other parent's house. In other words, you should not ask where they went, what they did, who they saw, etc., when with the other parent. You can ask how everything went, or if

103

they had a nice time, or if they ate. If information is volunteered, that is fine. If you are just given one word answers, don't push unless you believe there is an issue that is putting your teenager in a dangerous situation. If you believe, for example, that your child's other parent is allowing her/him to drink alcohol, abuse drugs, or engage in any other activity that you consider dangerous, you should address that to the court, with the assistance of your attorney, as soon as possible.

DECISIONS

When deciding how to handle issues concerning your children, it is crucial that you consider all the consequences of your decisions. When you agree to something in your divorce, it is likely going to become part of your Divorce Agreement. Your Divorce Agreement is the document that you are going to live by until your children are 18[22] or 21[23] years old, therefore you must be careful and deliberate about the decisions you make concerning your children. With regard to your children, your Divorce Agreement will include everything such as the days of the week that each parent will spend time with the children, which parent will spend time with the children on the various holidays, who will see the children on their birthdays and the amount of vacation time each child will have with each parent. Think of the consequences of every decision you make in your divorce. Failure to do so may have lasting devastating effects. Read what your FDW, John, has to say:

---

[22] Child support ends in most states at age 18 if the child is working full-time or is married or in the military.

[23] Child support ends in most states at the age of 21 if the child attends four consecutive years of college.

JOHN

When we went to court the first time, I was requesting custody of our daughter, Elizabeth, who was two years old, because I felt that my ex was too physically rough with her when she had temper tantrums. One example was that if my daughter had a temper tantrum, my ex would roughly pound her into her stroller. I also felt that my ex was careless when she was taking care of our daughter. She did not watch her closely and our daughter climbed out of her crib and broke her wrist. Despite all of that, when we went to court, I agreed to my ex having 50-50 custody because I just wanted to get it over with and settle. Plus, I was getting word from mutual friends that my ex was going to take my daughter and run to California and I thought I would never see her at all. At the time, I thought that the mother had all the rights, and the father had no chance of getting custody, even though my lawyer told me my chances were good. I was happy that I got 50% of the custody. I was like "Thank God for that". As time went by, my daughter complained more and more about abuse by her mother. Her mother would pull her hair and hit her and was verbally abusive to her. In retrospect, I could have seen that coming. I was sorry that I did not get custody of her when she was younger. I went back to court years later and had a long, drawn-out battle with her mother for custody. I finally got full custody of our daughter when she was 12 years old.

CUSTODY OF THE CHILDREN

The decisions that you make concerning custody of your children will have a lasting impact on their lives. The different types of custody vary from state to state, and you should speak with your attorney about the types of custody that are available in your state. In most states, the decision boils down to whether one parent will have physical custody, while the other parent has scheduled parenting time, or whether both parents will have an equal amount of parenting time with the child which is "50-50" custody.

For some divorcing couples, the custody decision is straightforward and agreed upon without conflict. For other couples, it is a decision which requires the court's assistance to resolve.

For example, you may not agree to your spouse's request for 50-50 custody because you are aware of your spouse's work schedule and believe that your spouse will not be home and the children will be cared for by someone else during his/her parenting time. While it is acceptable for either one of you to hire a babysitter if you will not be home for a short period of time, you may feel that your children would be more comfortable with one of their parents instead of a babysitter on most of the nights that the other parent has parenting time. In that situation it is best to have the parenting schedule adjusted so that the child can be with each parent when he/she is not working. If this cannot be agreed upon, it must be addressed in court.

Every situation is unique. For example, the medical and law enforcement fields have rotating work schedules that vary from week to week. An agreement for parents in those professions may stipulate the number of days per week the parent will have the child instead of the specific days of the week, since the days off will change from week to week. Your attorney will help you get through the details of the times and days of visitation.

50-50 custody works best if you and your spouse/former spouse get along well enough to talk about the children, live near each other, and the children have similar accommodations in both homes. Your goal is to make it as easy as possible for the children to go back-and-forth between both places. If you live near each other, getting them to school will be easier. If you live, for example, one hour away from each other, something like getting the children to school on time will be more difficult because they will have to wake up much earlier in the morning and they may not be able to take the school bus with their friends.

If you and your child's other parent do not get along, 50-50 custody will be logistically difficult. It is important for you and your spouse/former spouse to be able to discuss issues concerning the children and to be flexible. For example, if one of the children has a class trip and due to a work schedule one of you must drop the child off earlier or later to the other parent's house, there must be coordination and discussion. If you are not able to do these things, 50-50 custody will be complicated and hard on the children. Your goal is to make everything easy for the children. So, if they have things at both houses that make them comfortable and if there's no arguing in the presence of the children between pick up and drop off, then it's a more comfortable situation for the children.

If you are unable to agree about the type of custody each parent will have, your attorney will file the necessary papers in court so that the judge can decide. Once there is an agreement or decision concerning custody, it will become part of your Divorce Agreement and Judgment of Divorce. That custody order or agreement will remain in effect until there is a new court order. You therefore should make sure that this is a decision that you can live with, and more importantly, is in the best interests of your child.

PARENTAL ALIENATION/ALIENATED CHILD

Parental Alienation is a 1980s U.S. psychology term that *legal dictionary.net* defined in 2017 as: "The manipulation of a child to reject one parent or the other." As of 2020, *Wikipedia* expanded the definition of Parental Alienation as follows:

"Parental alienation describes a process through which a child becomes estranged from a parent as the result of the psychological manipulation of another parent.[24] [25] The child's estrangement may manifest itself as fear, disrespect or hostility toward the distant parent, and may extend to additional relatives or parties.[26] The child's estrangement is disproportionate to any acts or conduct attributable to the alienated parent.[27] Parental alienation can occur in any family unit, but is believed to occur most often within the context of family separation, particularly when legal proceedings are involved,[28] although the participation of professionals such as lawyers, judges and psychologists may also contribute to the conflict.[29]

The effects of alienated children[30] on families are devastating and often permanent. Unfortunately, although virtually all of the courts in the United States have rules and directives which provide that one parent should not disparage or speak negatively about the other parent to the children, it happens almost routinely in divorces. Parents going through divorce often state as justification for speaking negatively about their children's other parent that "they (the children) are old enough to know" or they are "just telling the truth" or that "they don't hide anything" from their children. They often further rationalize that the child "should know" what

---

[24] Jaffe, Alan, M.; Thakkar, Melanie J.; Piron, Pascale; Walla, Peter (11 May 2017). "Denial of ambivalence as a hallmark of parental alienation. *Cogent Psychology*.

[25] Kruk, Edward (2018). "Parental Alienation as a Form of Emotional Child Abuse: Current State of Knowledge and Future Directions for Research" *Family Science Review* 22 (4): 142.

[26] Doughty, Julie; Maxwell, Nina; Slater, Tom (April 2018). "Review of Research and case law on parental alienation". *ORCA-Online Research at Cardiff University*. Cascade Children's Social Care Research and Development Center. P. 21.

[27] Ellis, Elizabeth M.: Boyan, Susan (30 April 2010). "Intervention Strategies for Parent Coordinators in Parental Alienation Cases". *The American Journal of Family Therapy*. 38 (3): 218-236.

[28] Harman, Jennifer J.; Leder-Elder, Sadie; Biringen, Zeynep (July 2016). "Prevalence of parental alienation drawn from a representative poll". *Children and Youth Services Review*. 66: 62-66

[29] Braver, Sanford, L.: Cookston, Jeffrey T.; Cohen, Bruce R. (October 2002). "Experiences of Family Law Attorneys with Current Issues in Divorce Practice". Family Relations. 51 (4): 325-334.

[30] Kelly, J.B.; Johnston, J.R., *Family Court Review*, Vol. 39 No. 3, July 2001 249-266.

the other parent is doing and "make his/her own decision", but it's not that easy. Children love their parents and believe what they say. If one parent tells them something negative about the other parent, repeatedly, with emotion, they are very likely to believe it. The parent usually makes whatever they are saying sound very believable to the child, even if it is fabricated.

Subtle things that a parent says to a child about the other parent run deep. For example, if the parent says I would love to buy you this, but I can't because your father doesn't give us enough money, the child will likely become resentful against the father. He will wonder why his father is not giving his mother enough money. The child does not know whether the father is giving his mother the money that he was court ordered to pay for spousal support and child support. All the child knows is that mom said that dad is not giving mom enough money. The child has no reason to suspect that mom is not telling the truth. He loves his mom and believes her.

If, as another example, the father always asks the child when he/she visits, "Did your mom remember to do [this], because she always forgets?" Or if the child has a scraped knee or elbow and the father says, "How did you fall? Was your mom not being careful again?", the child will eventually start thinking that mom is not careful and might start telling mom that she always forgets everything or that she is not careful. Similarly, if the father, for example, constantly says that the mother is crazy, the child will start saying the same thing.

Surprisingly, the age of the children is not a factor in alienation. Adult children are just as easily influenced by a parent as younger children are. Below you will see two accounts by your FDWs of what happened to them.

RYAN

After we started the divorce, I was still living in the house with my wife and two daughters. She would say things to them to put ideas in their head that I was doing inappropriate things. Of a sexual nature. One night I was tucking my 10-year-old daughter into bed and kissing her goodnight on the forehead. My wife came to the bedroom door and said, "What are you doing?" I said, "Kissing Sally good night". My wife said "That's inappropriate. Sally, Dad shouldn't be smothering you with kisses. That's inappropriate". Stuff like that. One day I was tickling my other daughter, who was 8 years old, and my wife said "Why are you tickling her? That's inappropriate touching. Emily, Daddy's touching you inappropriately, you realize that, right?" It was crazy. She would say "Dad doesn't give me any money" "Dad is the one causing this". She would say some things that were true, like we are getting divorced or selling the house, but she would tell our daughters that it was because of me. She would also just make shit up. Whatever she could say just to put me in a bad light to the kids. It was a horror show. Just terrible.

TONY

My wife wanted a divorce. I didn't. I was shocked when she asked for one. I spoke to her about trying to work everything out. But she wouldn't change her mind. I had always been very close to my three sons during our marriage. I did everything with them. I coached their sports since the time they were little and continued when they went to high school and helped them all get scholarships for college. I was so close to them. Despite all of that, somehow my wife managed to convince them that I had been physically abusive to her. Something that was not even close to being true. My sons lived with us in the house. They knew that I was always telling them to be respectful to their mother. I never laid a hand on her. They never saw me lay hands on her. They weren't little kids. I couldn't understand how they would believe her. My youngest was in high school, one was in college and one had graduated from a top college and was working already. I thought they knew me. But they believed her. She made up lie after lie about me. She said that I hit her and beat her when they weren't around. And they believed it. They stopped talking to me. I tried over and over again to get them to see what the truth was. But they still believed her. Even though she said all of those horrible things about me to the children, I didn't say anything bad about her. I only told them that what she said about me wasn't true. I tried to spend time with my sons, but they refused most of the time. When they did spend time with me, it was short and fleeting. Even my youngest son in high school stopped spending time with me because he was so worried about what his mother would think. She would cry and tell him about these horrible things that I did to her which never happened and make him feel guilty if he spent any time with me. She would call the police if I came around to the house. One time I saw that the grass at the house was really high and the pool hadn't been opened for the summer, so I thought that I would surprise them and mow the lawn and take care of the pool for them so that my sons could enjoy it. Instead of being grateful, she called the police.

On another occasion, I traveled all the way to my son's college to watch him play in his game. Something that I always did during the marriage. My wife was there with her family and her father assaulted me. I went to court and I got an order of protection against her father. Instead of my children being mad at her father for assaulting me, they were mad at me for bringing the order of protection against him. Everything was twisted around to make it look like I was the one at fault. I was paying for everything and doing my best to have a relationship with my children, and I was made to be the bad guy. My wife ruined my relationship with my sons forever. I believe I am a strong man. I can hide my emotions and compartmentalize a lot, but this divorce brought me to my knees over my kids.

Alienation of children is hurtful, and it lasts a lifetime. The parent and the child lose relationships that are important to them. In rare cases, years later the child realizes that maybe what the other parent said was not true and they reunite with the alienated parent. But, in most cases, that relationship is forever destroyed.

Children who feel loved, safe and secure become well-adjusted and happier adults. Children who feel unloved or betrayed by one of their parents feel less safe and more insecure and have more issues as adults. Children of divorce should not be casualties. If you take care to allow your children to love both parents and keep your issues with your spouse private so that only the two of you handle them (with the assistance of the court when necessary) your children will be much happier and secure.

You usually learn that your spouse or former spouse is disparaging you to the children because of something the children say to you. You should always correct them and let them know what the truth is. For example, "Mom said that you moved out because you don't care about what happens to us." Your answer should be, "I love you very much and I do care what happens to you." Then you should discuss attending family therapy with your spouse. If your spouse doesn't agree, see if he/she will agree to counseling with a therapist for the child. If your spouse still does not agree, a therapist can be ordered by the judge. You should tell your attorney immediately if you learn that your child's other parent is saying negative things about you to the children. Your attorney will address the issue with your spouse's attorney and the court. Alienation of children can be stopped if it is caught early and addressed. If it is permitted to continue for months or years, the effects may be devastating and irreversible.

Allow your children to love their other parent, even if you don't. They will thank you for it.

CHILDREN WITH SPECIAL NEEDS

While most aspects of your divorce will be similar to those of typical divorcing couples, some of the issues involving special needs children are different. The term "special needs" describes a wide range of children. Some are physically disabled, some are neurologically impaired, some have cognitive deficiencies, while others have emotional or psychiatric disabilities. When deciding which parent will have physical custody of a special needs child, the child's medical and educational needs should be taken into consideration. The agreement should be as specific as possible concerning whom the child's caretakers will be while with each parent. It should include days of the week, times of day and location of the caretaker whenever possible. The more specific the agreement is, the easier it will be to enforce. It should also include information such as both parents having medications and equipment in their homes and directing that the child continue with the medications and therapies in each home. Routine and diet are often extremely important for special needs children, and a direction that the parents continue the agreed upon schedule and diet for the child in the Divorce Agreement or by court order, if necessary, should be put in place.

VALERIE

When you have special needs children, the fight to protect them, I suppose, is even more intense. They need protection in a way that typical children don't need it. My lawyer made sure to put provisions in the agreement that would protect the children after divorce. She also made sure that everyone knew that their needs were different from those of other children. She made sure my voice was heard. That made all the difference. If you have special needs children make sure that you don't have a cookie-cutter Divorce Agreement. Make sure it specifies what you need for your children now and what they will need in the future.

While typical children may become independent (or emancipated) at the ages of 18 or 21, special needs children may require care for longer. At the age of 18, a special needs child requires that a parent be appointed legal guardian to continue to make medical decisions for the child. To make the transition as conflict-free as possible, your divorce agreement should state who will be the primary legal guardian and who will be the secondary legal guardian. You may also choose to be co-guardians if your state permits that. The agreement should indicate whether the child may live in an institution or group home and the conditions for when that will occur. If there is a trust for the child which provides for the child's future care after the death of the parents, or which provides for the child's financial future, the divorce agreement should specifically refer to the trust. There should be a provision concerning how the child's medical expenses, that are not covered by health insurance, will be paid. There should also be a provision stating that the parties will cooperate if the child is to apply for a special needs trust or government benefits in the future. If you make sure your divorce agreement is tailored to the specific needs of your child, you will have peace of mind that your child will be protected and well cared for.

CHAPTER 10

DOMESTIC ABUSE

"Controllers, abusers and manipulative people don't question themselves.
They don't ask themselves if the problem is them.
They always say the problem is someone else."

-Darlene Ouimet

Domestic abuse is the cause of many divorces. But it often takes a long time for a victim of abuse to make the decision to get divorced. In the beginning he/she may feel that the abuse was an isolated incident that will get better over time or may rationalize that the abuse only occurs when their spouse is under the influence of a substance. The abuser is often nicer when not under the influence of a substance. Possibly still short-tempered, but nicer. The abuser usually has some redeeming qualities. It is not uncommon for abusers to have engaging personalities, be loved by their coworkers and have many friends. The only people who may know about the abuse are the abuser, the spouse who is the subject of the abuse and the children who live with them. Eventually, as the marriage continues, the verbal abuse might spill out in public. Physical abuse, however, often continues in private. Here are the experiences of two of your FDWs:

LYNNE

Throughout my marriage, my husband was verbally abusive. We had two children on the autism spectrum and he basically couldn't handle it. I did everything. I dealt with the abuse throughout the marriage. When I told him that I thought we should get divorced, he didn't like that. He grabbed me and threw me to the ground, which left me crawling to the phone to call 911. I obtained an Order of Protection against him. Then I filed for divorce. The divorce was very contested. He fought me on everything. He said that he wanted the house and custody of the children. He wanted to have the van which I used every day to take the children to school and their activities instead of the older car he normally drove. I had to fight with everything I had to keep our house so my children would stay in the only home they had known and give them security once I'm gone. He didn't really want any of those things. He's an abuser. It was all about control. We had to hire an attorney for the children to make sure their interests were protected. In the end we resolved everything. I was forced to spend thousands of dollars opposing his request for custody, even though I knew he really never wanted to have the children live with him. I have custody of our children and after all of that fighting, he has never really visited the children for the amount of time that he was given in the agreement.

SAMANTHA

When I met my ex, I thought that he was a decent guy. He was nice looking, and we got along great. But after we had our daughter, I found out that was not what he was like at all. He was emotionally and mentally abusive and alluded to the fact that he could be physical. I felt that he was dangerous. He had a fascination with guns and used intimidation tactics to scare me.

I remember that all I wanted to do was protect my daughter. She was still just a toddler. My attorney and I went to court so that I could get custody. My ex was very scary. I was shaking every time we went to court. My attorney arranged it so that I would stay in a special room in the courthouse for victims of domestic violence until our case was called because I was so worried that he would do something to me. He actually put up a website about how much he hated me. My attorney was a Pit Bull in a skirt! She was my voice. She spoke for me. I gave her the information, and she told the judge what I was too nervous to say for myself. She would get me prepared before every court appearance. She explained to me after each court appearance what happened and what our next steps were. I always felt protected when I went to court. My attorney would even have the court officer walk us outside and she would walk me to the car also just to make sure I got there safely. That made all the difference. I got custody of my daughter and she's amazing and great and, most of all, safe and happy.

If you're the victim of abuse and you're reading this book, I commend you because it's a very difficult decision and a huge step to get a divorce. There are varying degrees of abuse: verbal, mental, emotional, sexual, physical, and threatened physical abuse. If you're in a situation where if your spouse finds out that you are planning to leave, you think your spouse may attempt to kill or severely hurt you, simply announcing that you would like a divorce is dangerous. You must plan to get away from your spouse safely before telling him/her about the divorce. Here is a link to all of the domestic violence agencies throughout the country, as well as two national phone numbers for victims of domestic violence: https://www.womenslaw.org/find-help/advocates-and-shelters

National Domestic Violence Hotline – 1-800-799-SAFE (7233) or TTY 1-800-787-3224
National Sexual Assault Hotline – (800) 656-HOPE

You should contact one of the above advocates, as well as an attorney, before you let your spouse know that you are contemplating divorce. There are even strategies for you to leave and obtain a new identity if you believe that you are in danger of your spouse trying to kill you. The domestic violence agencies will know how to help you and get you to a safe house. Many agencies will assist you in obtaining an attorney to help you get the court orders that you require to be protected.

While physical abuse may occur inconsistently at various times throughout an abusive marriage, verbal abuse is usually constant and more severe in times of stress. If you are being physically abused by your spouse, you should call the police whenever it happens. This would include even if your spouse was threatening you, throwing something at you or punching a hole in the wall while attempting to strike you. This is important because if the police come, they will give you a written report documenting what occurred. If your spouse assaults you, resulting in signs of abuse on your body such as a bruise or a broken bone, the police will likely arrest and remove your spouse from the marital residence.

If your spouse injures you and you require medical attention, obtain copies of the medical records as well. If you are physically abused and have a mark on your body such as a bruise, take a picture of it. Even if you decide not to get a divorce at that time, you will have proof of what transpired during the marriage. When you decide to get divorced, if there has been continued abuse, those photographs, medical records, and police reports will be used as evidence if you seek an order of protection from the court.

If the abuse has extended to your children, you should call Child Protective Services. Here is a link for all the child protection agencies in the country:

https://www.childwelfare.gov/organizations/?CWIGFunctionsac tion=rols:main.dspList&rolType=custom&rs_id=5.

The child protection agency will investigate and determine whether the allegation of abuse is substantiated. Be aware that *you should not falsely accuse* your spouse of abuse in an attempt to obtain an advantage in the divorce. The truth will come out. And if your accusations cannot be substantiated, it may diminish your credibility in court.

If there was verbal abuse during the marriage, even if there was no physical abuse, your spouse may be very difficult to deal with during the divorce. Your spouse may fight you on issues that are illogical based on the circumstances, like what happened to Lynne. For example, your spouse may illogically fight for custody of the children despite a work schedule that makes taking care of them virtually impossible. Abuse is about control. That's all it is. In many cases, your abusive spouse will continue abusive behavior during the divorce by fighting for the things (such as custody, the marital residence or your fair share of the marital assets) that are important to you. This may make you nervous when you go to court. Your abuser may laugh at you when you walk by, make a hurtful or vulgar comment while you are in earshot, or lie about you to the judge. This is all an effort to unnerve and intimidate you. A strategy that I have suggested to my clients over the years that has proven very beneficial, is to picture your abuser as a CARTOON CHARACTER. You know everything that they will do. You know, for example, that they will be late for court, or that they will make faces at you or that they will laugh while you are speaking. Whenever they do any of those things, you say to yourself "total cartoon character!". This way, instead of getting upset, you have a chuckle to yourself. Here is how your FDW, Lisa, used that strategy:

LISA

During our marriage, my ex-husband was physically and verbally abusive to me. We got divorced, which wasn't easy, but we got it done. After the divorce, my ex-husband continued to be abusive by doing things that he knew would hurt me, just to interrupt my life. There were times that he would sleep across the street from our home just to watch and make sure I wasn't dating anyone. It was so frightening and unsettling. He would come to our children's sporting events and berate them from the sideline. There was one particular time that he walked by me and threw his shoulder into me and almost knocked me to the ground. I had to call the police and have them come to the field. I was distraught, and it was very embarrassing. It was one of the many orders of protection I would obtain against him. I remember one day after I was remarried and living in my new house with my new husband and children in a beautiful neighborhood, he came to pick up the children, which should have been routine and uneventful. Instead he got there earlier than he was supposed to, pulled into our driveway, and started repeatedly blowing the car horn. We ran outside to see what was going on. The kids weren't ready yet because he was early. He started yelling loudly that I better get the kids out to his car. That he had a court order. That he was going to call the police. The children were scared and embarrassed. The neighbors could hear him. I had to calm them down and still send them with their father. As time went on, he would harass my new husband and me at sporting events or follow me around in stores. I would be so nervous whenever we went to court because he would continuously lie about me to the judge. He made up stories that I would somehow instigate him, which I would have never done. He was always late to court. His attorney was always late. And his attorney would always talk about me and to me in such a vile way. She would say my name like she was saying something disgusting and poisonous. It was upsetting to me. My attorney calmed me down by telling me to picture my husband and his attorney as cartoon characters. We did that for the judge too. The cartoon character images helped ease my mind and made me laugh to myself. It helped make my stressful court appearances more tolerable.

If you have a valid claim and your spouse is abusive, you should not just give in to his/her demands to avoid dealing with him/her. Provide the court with the necessary proof to substantiate your claims, protect your children and yourself, and obtain financial support as well as your fair share of the marital assets.

In some states, abuse is a factor to consider when dividing the marital assets. In other words, if a spouse is proven to have been abusive during the marriage, the abuser will be denied his/her share of the victim's assets. Your attorney will be able to advise you as to whether this factor applies in your state.

Going through a divorce with an abusive spouse is difficult, but not impossible. You take it one step at a time and *work with your attorney* to prove what you must to achieve your goals and objectives. Persevere, and you will make it successfully through your D.J. to your new A.D. life.

CHAPTER 11

HELLO??? ARE YOU LISTENING?

"When someone shows you who they are, believe them the FIRST time."

- Maya Angelou

SHEILA

I went to court for custody of my children. I initially represented myself because I couldn't afford an attorney. Then the court appointed an attorney for me. I called that lawyer so many times before my next court date. I left him messages, but he never called me back. That made me feel like I was nothing. Like I didn't count. Like my problems didn't mean anything. I had no idea what to do when that happened. It was horrible.

What if you do everything right? You get a word-of-mouth referral for an attorney, you provide your attorney with all the information required to prove your case, but it just seems like the attorney is not listening to you. You call the office, but your call is not returned. You try to make an appointment and the office says that they will call you back to schedule it, then they never call. When you finally meet in person, the attorney does not seem to be interested or agree with the issues you believe are important. Or the attorney expresses agreement with you, but in court does not correctly or adequately convey your issues to the judge. What do you do? Are you stuck with that attorney forever? Do you have to just deal with it even though you feel like it's not going well? The answer to the question is "NO"! If you feel that your attorney doesn't listen or is not interested in the issues you believe are important, without explanation, then that is a breakdown in communication. Your attorney is supposed to be your voice and your advocate when you go to court. If he/she is not listening to you, and your objectives and concerns are not being communicated to the court, *you have the right to obtain a new attorney.* There should always be clear communication between you and your attorney, and you should be satisfied that your attorney is either attempting to achieve your objectives or explaining the reasons why your objectives might not be accomplished. If your attorney is not responding to your phone calls or emails, then contact the office and make an appointment. When you have that in-person meeting with your attorney, be clear about what it is that you wish to discuss. Write down all the points you want to discuss and what your goal is for that meeting. For example, if there's a court appearance coming up, find out what's happening at that next court appearance. If you were supposed to be meeting with your spouse and his/her attorney to discuss settlement, find out whether it has been scheduled and what discussions have taken place between the attorneys.

There may be legitimate reasons why your attorney is not able to meet your objectives. When you meet with your attorney, ask what is being done to achieve your objectives. Request an explanation of the status of your case. The wheels of justice turn slowly. The attorney may be working towards your objectives, even if they have not yet been achieved. Sometimes what you desire is not able to be achieved based on the law, or the particular facts of your case. If the communication with your attorney is good, he/she will explain how the law affects your particular situation, so you do not expect a result that is unrealistic or unlikely. If you are unable to communicate with your attorney, and you feel that you do not understand what is happening in your own divorce, or the attorney does not give you an explanation, then you should hire a different attorney. When you initiate the search for a new attorney, use the checklist that we discussed in Chapter 2 under the subheading "How to Choose". That should help to ensure that you choose the right attorney for you.

When you go to the new attorney for the interview, bring all the court orders and all the papers that you have so far in your court case. You should get a copy of your file from your current attorney. Make sure that you have everything. Most attorneys will require you to pay whatever outstanding money you owe them before they give you the file. Depending on what state you are in and what your retainer agreement says, this may or may not be legal. You may request that your new attorney advise you about obtaining your file from your former attorney.

You should be prepared to pay the attorney you are leaving any money that you owe, so that you may move forward with your new attorney. When you interview the potential new attorney, ask that your court and other divorce documents be reviewed and request an explanation of what would be done differently from your current attorney. If the attorney agrees with what your current attorney is doing and states that you may not have a different outcome, but you will have better communication and be more in the loop, you may feel more comfortable with the new attorney when you're going to court. If you decide to switch attorneys, your new attorney will have you complete paperwork that will be sent to your former attorney, your spouse's attorney and the court to notify them of the change and permit you to obtain your file from the former attorney.

CHAPTER 12

GOING BACK TO COURT
A.D. (AFTER DIVORCE)

"It's time to face the music."

- Author unknown

Is everything over once you get your Judgment of Divorce? The answer is "it depends". Your Judgment of Divorce and your Divorce Agreement are contracts that you and your former spouse must follow concerning your children, your finances and division of debts/assets. If you divided retirement assets, the court usually requires a separate court order that is provided to the retirement plan, in order to divide it. In many courts, the Judgment of Divorce is an exhibit that must be attached to the request for the order dividing up your retirement plans. After you get your Judgment of Divorce, you should be aware of all the things that have to take place after you receive it. For example, you may have to change your health insurance if you are no longer covered by your spouse's health insurance.

If your spouse does not follow the agreement by paying you the child support and/or spousal support that you're supposed to receive, or if you have not received your share of the marital assets, you can return to court to enforce the agreement. Therefore, it is very important for you to *keep good records*. If possible, have child support automatically deducted from your spouse's salary to ensure that you receive it. Most states have support collection units that will garnish the child support from your spouse's salary, so you should ask your attorney about getting that put into place for you. If you decide not to go that route, keep records of when your spouse pays you. Insist that he/she pays by check. If you are the one paying support, pay by check so that you have proof that you are making the child support and spousal support payments. Keep a record of all the payments that you make, including payments for extracurricular activities, education, or tuition for college. This is important because if you are brought back to court by your spouse and accused of not making payments, you will have proof that the payments were made. If you bring your former spouse to court for failure to make payments to you, you will have proof of the payments that were not made. If your spouse is supposed to be paying for extracurricular activities such as dance lessons or karate, obtain an invoice on the official letterhead of the company providing the lesson so that you have proof of the bill. Your payment by check will be the proof that you paid it. All communication with your spouse asking for payment should be by email or text message so that you have proof of the request.

If the issue is with regard to custody or visitation, keep records about what's going on. You should know your Divorce Agreement well. Make sure that you have everything you need in order to prove your position before you go back to court. If possible, call your attorney when there's an issue to talk it through to see if it's something that's worth going to court about and whether it makes economic sense to do so.

OLIVIA

> *My ex-husband and I had a very contested divorce. He fought me on everything, including custody of our daughter. It was very difficult, but in the end, I was able to get custody of my daughter. Because my husband was abusing drugs, he was ordered to only see my daughter with supervision. He refused to do that and instead just never visited our daughter. He was also always behind on his child support. We went back to court to enforce the court-ordered child support, but he never had the money. He was in and out of rehabs. It was a very difficult situation. Even though he was given many chances, he chose not to see our daughter. I remarried years after our divorce. My new husband was the father that my ex-husband never was to our daughter. She hadn't seen her father in years. He didn't even call her. It was actually really sad. Even though I put it off for a while, I finally went to court. Once we were in court, my ex-husband agreed to relinquish custody. It was hard to go back to court, but in the end, it was the best thing we ever did for our daughter. My new husband adopted my daughter and we have a beautiful happy family together now.*

As you can see from what Olivia shared, going back to court after you have finally completed your divorce is a difficult decision. It brings back difficult memories and has a financial impact. Yet, once you go and are able to enforce your agreement, you are usually gratified and empowered. You worked hard to get your agreement. Know it and ask the court to enforce it when necessary.

AFTERWORD

Before you read, *You're Getting Divorced...Now What?* you had questions and concerns about what your next steps should be once the reality that you are getting divorced sunk in. Now that you've read the book, you know that you're not alone, the emotions you are feeling are normal, and you know how to choose a lawyer. You are now empowered because you are aware of the realities of the cost of a divorce, you know what to say and what not to say to the children, and you have important information concerning situations including financial support, the marital residence, safety of your children, substance abuse, mental illness, alienated children and domestic violence. You have been given the tools to plan for court and your divorce journey and you have a feeling of confidence because the processes you learned prepared you for each step of your journey. You even know what to do if your attorney is not working with you to obtain your main objectives and you have information about going back to court to enforce orders after your divorce is completed.

Your FDWs are standing with you as you go through your D.J. and will be there until you reach your new A.D. life.

You can do this! Your new life is waiting for you on the other side of your divorce.

GLOSSARY

A.D. – After Divorce.

Alienated child – Alienated child-child who freely and persistently expresses unreasonable negative feelings and beliefs (such as anger, hatred, rejection, and/or fear) toward a parent that are disproportionate to their actual experience with that parent.

Attorney – *Attorney* and *lawyer* are synonyms and are used interchangeably.

Attorney Fees Formula - Hourly Rate (*$*) multiplied by Number of Hours (#) = Total Retainer Fee (*$$*).

B.D. – Before Divorce.

Buyout – When one spouse is paid money by the other spouse for his/her share of marital property.

Conference – Meeting with the attorneys and the court about the status of divorce and the ability to resolve your issues.

Contested Divorce – when two spouses in a divorce do not agree on most issues.

Court Appearance – Any time that you go to court and meet with the judge.

Credibility – the quality of being trusted and believed.

Court Transcript – the word for word typewritten recording of everything that was said during your court appearance.

50-50 Custody – When the children live with each parent for an equal amount of time.

Disparage – to make negative statements about another person.

Divorce Agreement – The final document at the completion of the divorce that contains all the terms and conditions that the parties must follow.

D.J. – Divorce Journey.

Equity Formula – Value of House (V) minus Mortgage Balance (M) = Equity in the house (E).

Evidence – Testimony supported by documentation.

FDW – Fellow Divorce Warrior.

Government Benefits – Social security disability, Medicare, Medicaid.

Hair Follicle Test – a hair drug screen test that screens for illicit drug use and the misuse of prescription medications. During this test, a small amount of hair is removed using scissors. The sample is then analyzed. The analysis can detect substances for up to 90 days depending on the length of the hair sample.

Hearing – when the court hears testimony from witnesses and accepts evidence about limited issues in your divorce.

Instant Test – uses urine or saliva to test for the presence of substances.

Judgment of Divorce – the legal document signed by a judge that renders you divorced.

Lawyer – *Lawyer* and *attorney* are synonyms and are used interchangeably.

Legal Guardian – a person who has been court appointed to care for another person and make decisions on their behalf.

Marital Asset – anything purchased during the marriage with marital money.

Marital Money – any money earned during the marriage.

Marital Residence – where husband and wife resided during the marriage.

Motion – a request to the court for some type of relief such as temporary custody, child support or spousal support while your divorce is pending. Motions may also be made after your divorce to enforce a Court order.

NBC – Do not say anything Negative about your child's other parent. Do not Blame the other parent for your situation. Do not share with the children what is occurring in Court.

Parental Alienation – A process through which a child becomes estranged from a parent due to psychological manipulation by another parent, often in the context of family separation and legal proceedings.

Parenting Time – visitation time that the child has with the parent.

Post Traumatic Stress Disorder – anxiety and flashbacks caused by a traumatic event.

Primary Custodial Parent - the parent that the child will live with for the majority of the week.

Process Server – a person, especially a sheriff or deputy, who serves (hand delivers) legal papers on a person.

Glossary

Proof – evidence.

P.T.S.D. – Post Traumatic Stress Disorder.

Random Testing – drug testing of an individual on short notice.

Retainer Formula - Hourly Rate (*$*) multiplied by Number of Hours (*#*) = Total Retainer Fee (*$$*).

Special Needs Trust – synonymous with Supplemental Needs Trust. A specialized trust that allows a disabled person to continue to receive government benefits.

Substances – illicit drugs, prescription narcotics, or alcohol.

Supplemental Needs Trust – synonymous with Special Needs Trust. A specialized trust that allows a disabled person to continue to receive government benefits.

Trial – when the court hears testimony from witnesses and accepts evidence about all the issues in your divorce.

Trust – a method of holding property or money for the benefit of others.

RESOURCES

1. Link for all the Courts in the United States of America: https://www.ncsc.org/information-and-resources/ state-court-websites

2. Link for all the legal aid programs in the United States of America: https://www.ncsc.org/topics/legal-services/ legal-aid-pro-bono/resource-guide

3. Link for all of the Bar Associations in the United States: https://generalbar.com/State.aspx

4. Link for all of the child protective services agencies in the United States is: https://www.childwelfare.gov/organizations

5. Link to all the domestic violence agencies throughout the country and two national phone numbers for victims of domestic violence: https://www.womenslaw.org/find-help/ advocates-and-shelters

6. National Domestic Violence Hotline – 1-800-799-SAFE (7233) or TTY 1-800-787-3224

7. National Sexual Assault Hotline – (800) 656-HOPE

8. Link for all the child protective services in the country:

9. Link for all the child protective services in the country: https://www.childwelfare.gov/organizations/?CWIGFunct ionsaction=rols:main.dspList&rolType=custom&rs_id=5

10. Police – call 911.

LINKS FOR FORMS

1. **GET YOUR MIND RIGHT©**
   www.radnalaw.com/YGDNW/forms/GetYourMindRight

2. **MY REASONS©**
   www.radnalaw.com/YGDNW/forms/MyReasons

3. **INITIAL PLAN©**
   www.radnalaw.com/YGDNW/forms/InitialPlan

4. **LAWYER PHONE CHECKLIST©**
   www.radnalaw.com/YGDNW/forms/LawyerPhoneChecklist

5. **LAWYER CONSULT PREP©**
   www.radnalaw.com/YGDNW/forms/LawyerConsultPrep

6. **CONSULT CHECKLIST©**
   www.radnalaw.com/YGDNW/forms/ConsultChecklist

7. **INTERIM PLAN©**
   www.radnalaw.com/YGDNW/forms/InterimPlan

8. **COURT PREP©**
   www.radnalaw.com/YGDNW/forms/CourtPrep

9. **OUT OF POCKET EXPENSE TRACKER©**
   www.radnalaw.com/YGDNW/forms/
   OutOfPocketExpenseTracker

10. **COURT QUESTIONS©**
    www.radnalaw.com/YGDNW/forms/CourtQuestions

11. **MENTAL ILLNESS©**
    www.radnalaw.com/YGDNW/forms/Mental-Illness

12. **SUBSTANCE ABUSE©**
    www.radnalaw.com/YGDNW/forms/SubstanceAbuse

ACKNOWLEDGEMENTS

Thank you to:

My clients who put their trust in me and whom I have had the privilege to assist through difficult situations. I have learned from you, been inspired by you, cried with you, and laughed with you. With many of you I have had the privilege to continue our relationship in your A.D. life, and for that I am always grateful.

My parents, Peter and Violette Radna, who modeled the empathy that I always strive to have for my clients. You taught me to look at each situation from the perspective of the other person, and I have done my best to pass that lesson on to my family and my staff.

My brother, Tony Radna, who has shown me that nothing is impossible.

My husband, Billy, who is my biggest cheerleader, greatest confidant, closest friend, and an amazing editor. You make everything I do easier, and I appreciate that every day.

My children, Ed and Pete who lift me up, inspire me, make me laugh, support me and who, along with my husband, were the first readers and excellent editors of this book. You make me proud always.

To my staff at Law Offices of Sandra M. Radna, P.C.: Nicole L. Scherer, Esq., Kathy Ann Wolverton, Esq., Briana Iannacci, Esq., who were early readers of this book and Kimberly Koehler, Ronni Sue Sarisky, Maureen Henry, Fran Beneventin, Heather Falco, Erin Michel, Elena O'Donnell and Gabriella Leon, Esq., who were all enthusiastic supporters of my endeavor to write this book. Thank you for all that you do that enables me to do what I do.

To my friends and colleagues throughout many industries who have been so kind and generous in their support of me through my book writing journey, with a special thanks to Christy Smith, Ed Scheine, Esq., Mike Quigley, Ralph Benzakien, Denise Angiulo, Ellen Volpe, Donna Drake, Lisa Mirabile, Jonathan Gassman, Yvonne Cort, Nikolay Afanasyev, Dolly Hertz and Bill Mountzouros. Your amazing ideas and words of encouragement with regard to writing this book have moved me forward and mean the world to me.

To Fred Dunwoody of FJD Associates, Inc. for his assistance in the finalization of the forms I created for use with this book.

To everyone at Ultimate 48 Hour Author and Ultimate World Publishing, with a special thanks to Natasa Denman, Stuart Denman, Vivienne Mason, my editor Hayley Ward and my book cover designer Nikola Boskovski, who helped me across the finish line of writing this book with your excellent processes and clear direction. Thank you, thank you, thank you!

ABOUT THE AUTHOR

S andra M. Radna, Esq. is an award-winning New York attorney
and the owner of Law Offices of Sandra M. Radna, PC. which
has offices in Manhattan and Long Island. Since 1993, she has
represented people going through divorce. She enjoys passionately
advocating for her clients to solve their legal issues even when the
odds seem insurmountable.

Sandra was selected as the top 1% of Family Lawyers by the
National Institute of Trial Lawyers; was interviewed by National
Public Radio (NPR) concerning the changes to tax laws that
affected alimony/maintenance payment deductions, has been
selected as one of the top Family and Divorce Lawyers by Long
Island Business News for five consecutive years and was selected
as a Lawyer of Distinction in the areas of Divorce and Family Law
as recognized by the New York Times and USA Today. Sandra
was a speaker at the National Conference of CPA Practitioners
on the issue of Divorce and Innocent Spouse and has also been
featured in Newsday concerning common law marriage.

Sandra is married, has two sons and lives on Long Island in New
York.

MORE PRAISE FOR
YOU'RE GETTING DIVORCED...NOW WHAT?

"You're Getting Divorced...Now What? is so helpful for anyone going through a contested divorce. Just having the YGDNW forms provided in the book make it an invaluable resource!"
— Beatrice Baron, *Grateful mother of two*

NOTES

CPSIA information can be obtained
at www.ICGtesting.com
Printed in the USA
FSHW021933250820
73264FS